Make - Up & Skin - Care

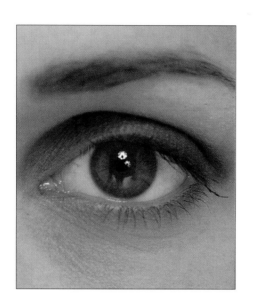

MAKE-UP &
SKIN-CARE

Natural Ways to a Perfect Complexion

Sally Norton

Photographs by Nick Cole
Make-up & Hair by Debbi Finlow

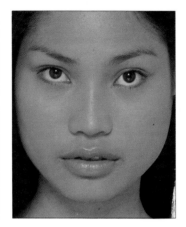

Sebastian Kelly

To George

This edition published in 1998 by Sebastian Kelly
2 Rectory Road, Oxford OX4 1BW

© Anness Publishing Limited 1996

Produced by Anness Publishing Limited
Hermes House, 88-89 Blackfriars Road
London SE1 8HA

ISBN 1-901688-65-8

A CIP catalogue record for this book is available from the British Library

Publisher: Joanna Lorenz
Project Editor: Sylvie Wootton
Designer: Patrick McLeavey

Printed and bound in Singapore by Star Standard Pte. Ltd.

1 3 5 7 9 10 8 6 4 2

ACKNOWLEDGEMENTS
Extra special thanks go to Debbi Finlow and Nick Cole for their close collaboration on
this book. Also, thanks to fashion stylist Dawn Clayton for all her help.
With special thanks to the following companies for providing beauty products for
photography: The Body Shop, Boots, Bourjois, Crabtree & Evelyn, Cutex, Elancyl,
L'Oreal, Rimmel and Sensiq. Photographs page 65, courtesy of Nivea. Additional thanks
to the following companies for their loan of clothing and accessories for photography:
Whistles, French Connection, Marks & Spencer, Descamps, Bhs, Debenhams, Fenwicks,
Adrien Mann, Knickerbox, Freemans.

Contents

INTRODUCTION 6

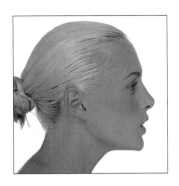

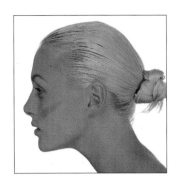

INTRODUCTION

This book is for every woman who is interested in beauty, skin-care and make-up. My aim is to show you that it's not only Supermodels and Hollywood actresses who can look wonderful. Every woman can make the most of her looks by learning the tricks of the trade, overcoming particular beauty problems and perfecting a look that really suits her. I've tried to peel away the mystique that commonly surrounds the world of make-up, skin-care and beauty products. The reality is that you can identify your special beauty needs to create tailormade regimes and a make-up look to suit you. Every woman is different, but by analysing what works for you, you'll save time, money and effort while looking better that you ever have before.

Most of us simply aren't able to spend hours in front of the mirror. That's why I believe it's important to master the basics and understand the products you're using. This way you'll always be able to put together an effortless look, because you'll know exactly the result you're trying to achieve.

I've also put together a battery of tricks, tips and special techniques to help you care for your skin and body and apply cosmetics like a professional make-up artist. It all adds up to a complete make-up, body and skin-care guide. I hope it inspires you to try something new, and that you enjoy using the book.

Sally Norton

BEAUTIFUL SKIN

Clear, soft and supple skin is one of the greatest beauty assets. While your actual skin-type is determined by your genes, there's plenty you can do on a day-to-day basis to ensure it always looks as good as possible. Understanding how your skin functions will awaken you to its special needs. In this section, we'll show you the perfect products and techniques to care for your own specific skin-type. Strategic and simple care on a daily basis will pay beautiful dividends. You can't neglect your complexion for months or years, then make up for it with expensive and intensive attention in the short term. You'll reap the benefits by regularly spending time and care on your skin. It's never too early or too late to follow a good skin-care regime – because the results will last a lifetime.

WHAT IS SKIN?

The dermis

The dermis is the layer that lies underneath the epidermis, and it is composed entirely of living cells. It consists of bundles of tough fibres which give your skin its elasticity, firmness and strength. There are also blood vessels, which feed vital nutrients to these areas.

Whereas the epidermis can usually repair itself and make itself as good as new, the dermis will be permanently damaged by injury.

The dermis also contains the following specialized organs:

Sebaceous glands are tiny organs which usually open into hair follicles on the surface of your skin. They produce an oily secretion, called sebum, which is your skin's natural lubricant.

The sebaceous glands are most concentrated on the scalp and face – particularly around the nose, cheeks, chin and forehead, which is why these are usually the most oily areas of your skin.

Left: Understanding your skin the way a beauty therapist would allows you to give it the care it deserves and to appreciate why certain factors are good for it – and others are not.
Below: Young or old, everyone's skin has the same basic structure.

Skin is your body's largest organ, covering every single surface of your body. Every woman can have beautiful skin no matter what her age, race or colouring. The secret is to understand how your skin functions, and how to treat it correctly.

TAKING A CLOSER LOOK

Your skin is made up of two main layers, called the epidermis and the dermis.

The epidermis

This is the top layer of skin and the one you can actually see. It protects your body from invasion and infection and helps to seal in moisture. It's built up of several layers of living cells which are then topped by sheets of dead cells. It's constantly growing, with new cells being produced at its base. They quickly die, and are pushed up to the surface by the arrival of new ones. These dead cells eventually flake away, which means that every new layer of skin is another chance to have a soft, glowing complexion.

The lower levels of living cells are fed by the blood supply from underneath, whereas the upper dead cells only need water to ensure they're kept plump and smooth.

The epidermis is responsible for your colouring, as it holds the skin's pigment. Its thickness varies, from area to area. For instance, it's much thicker on the soles of your feet than on your eyelids.

Above: Your skin is a sensor of pain, touch and temperature, offering protection and a means of eliminating waste.

Above: Your skin can cleanse, heal and even renew itself. How effectively it does these things is partly governed by you.

Above: Skin is a barometer of your emotions. It becomes red when you're embarrassed and quickly shows the signs of stress.

Sweat glands are all over your body. There are millions of them and their main function is to regulate your body temperature. When sweat evaporates on the skin's surface, the temperature of your skin drops.

Hairs grow from the hair follicles. They can help keep your body warm by trap-ping air underneath them. There are no hairs on the soles of your feet and palms of your hands.

THE MAIN FUNCTIONS OF YOUR SKIN

1 It acts as a thermostat, retaining heat or cooling you down with sweat.

2 It offers protection from potentially harmful things.

3 It acts as a waste disposal. Certain waste is expelled from your body 24 hours a day through your skin.

4 It provides you with a sense of touch, to help you communicate with the outside world.

Right: The condition of your skin is an overall sign of your health. It reveals stress, a poor diet and a lack of sleep. Taking care of your health will benefit your skin.

WHAT'S YOUR SKIN-TYPE?

There's no point spending a fortune on expensive skin-care products if you buy the wrong ones for your skin-type and collect yourself an assortment of discarded bottles. The key to developing a skin-care regime that works for you is to analyze your skin-type first.

SKIN-CARE QUIZ

To develop a better understanding of your skin and what will suit it best, start by answering the questions here. Then add up your score and check the list at the end to discover which of the skin-types you fit into.

1 How does your skin feel if you cleanse it with facial wash and water?
A Tight, as though it's too small for your face.
B Smooth and comfortable.
C Dry and itchy in places.
D Fine – quite comfortable.
E Dry in some areas and smooth in others.

2 How does your skin feel if you cleanse it with cream cleanser?
A Relatively comfortable.
B Smooth and comfortable.
C Sometimes comfortable, sometimes itchy.
D Quite oily.
E Oily in some areas and smooth in others.

3 How does your skin usually look by midday?
A Flaky patches appearing.
B Fresh and clean.
C Flaky patches and some redness.
D Shiny.
E Shiny in the T-zone.

4 How often do you break out in spots?
A Hardly ever.
B Occasionally, perhaps before or during your period.
C Occasionally.
D Often.
E Often – in the T-zone.

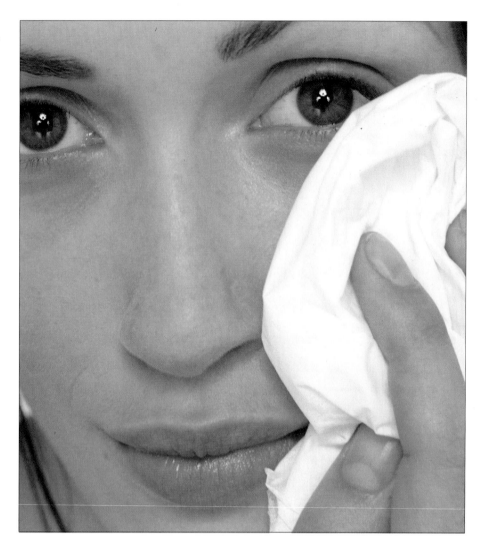

5 How does your skin react when you use facial toner?
A It stings.
B No problems.
C Stings and itches.
D Feels fresher.
E Feels fresher in some areas but stings in others.

6 How does your skin react to a rich night cream?
A It feels very comfortable.
B Comfortable.
C Sometimes feels comfortable, other times feels irritated.
D Makes my skin feel very oily.
E Oily in the T-zone, and comfortable on the cheeks.

Above: You know best how your skin reacts to different things so check your skin-type before you buy lots of skin-care products. Even if you you've been told what your skin-type is at some stage it is a good idea to run through this quiz now as you skin will change over a period of time.

Now add up your A's, B's, C's, D's and E's. Your skin-type is the one which has the majority of answers.
Mostly A's: Your skin is DRY.
Mostly B's: Your skin is NORMAL.
Mostly C's: Your skin is SENSITIVE.
Mostly D's: Your skin is OILY.
Mostly E's: Your skin is COMBINATION.

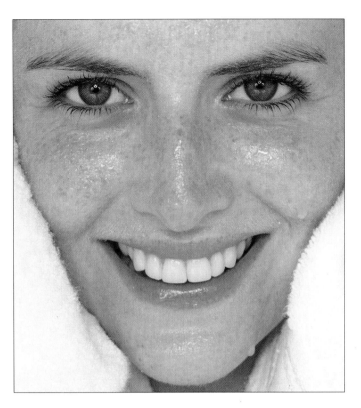

Is traditional soap and water cleansing for you?

Or is the gentle touch a softer option?

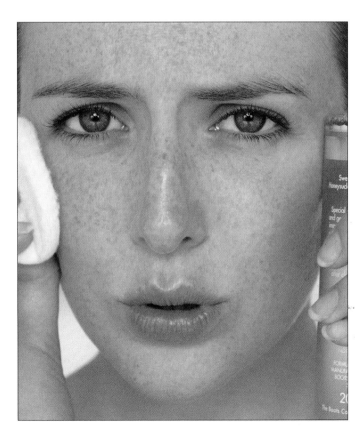

Do toners make your skin sting?

Are your face creams an embarrassment of riches?

THE TOP 10 SKIN-CARE PRODUCTS

Before you can devise the best regime for yourself and give your skin some special care, you need to understand what the main skin-care products are designed to do.

THE KEY TREATMENTS

From a basic soap and water cleansing routine, today's skin-care ranges have evolved into a sophisticated selection.

Facial washes

These liquids are designed to be lathered up with water to dissolve grime, dirt and stale make-up from the skin's surface.

Cleansing bars

Ordinary soap is too drying for most skins. However, now you can foam up with these special bars which will cleanse your skin without stripping it of moisture. They're refreshing for oilier skin-types, and help keep pores clear and prevent pimples and blackheads.

Cream cleansers

These are a wonderful way to cleanse drier complexions. They generally have quite a light, fluid consistency to make them easy to spread onto the skin. They contain oils to dissolve surface dirt and make-up, so they can be easily swept from your skin with cottonwool (cotton). Use damp cottonwool (cotton) if you prefer a fresher finish.

Toners and astringents

Designed to refresh and cool your skin, they quickly evaporate after being applied to the skin with cottonwool (cotton). They can also remove excess oil from the surface layers of your skin. The word "astringent" on the bottle means it has a higher alcohol content, and is only suitable for oily skins. The words "tonic" and "toner" mean that they're useful for normal or combination skins as they are gentler. Those with dry and sensitive skins should usually avoid these products as they can be too drying. Generally, if the product stings your face, move onto a gentler formulation or weaken it by adding a few drops of distilled water (available from a pharmacist).

Moisturizers

The key function of a moisturizer is to form a barrier film on the surface of your skin and prevent moisture loss from the top layers. This makes the skin feel softer and smoother. Generally, the drier your skin the thicker the moisturizer you should choose. All skin types need a moisturizer.

Moisturizers today also contain a myriad of other ingredients to treat your skin. The most valuable one to look for is a UV filter. With this your moisturizer will give your skin year-round protection from the ageing and burning rays of the sun.

Eye make-up removers

Ordinary cleansers aren't usually sufficient to remove stubborn eye make-up, which is why these products are so useful. If you wear waterproof mascara check that the product you use is designed to remove it.

SPECIAL TREATMENTS

In addition to a basic wardrobe of skin-care products, you can add a few extras.

Face masks

These are intensive treatments, designed either to deep cleanse your skin or dramatically boost its moisture levels.

Facial scrubs and exfoliaters

These creams or gels contain hundreds of tiny abrasive particles. When massaged into damp skin, these particles dislodge dead surface skin cells, revealing the younger, fresher cells underneath.

Eye creams

The delicate skin around your eyes is usually the first to show the signs of ageing. These gels and creams contain special ingredients to plump out fine lines, and keep this skin soft. They can also help reduce puffiness and under eye shadows.

Night creams

These are intensive creams, designed to give your skin extra pampering while you sleep. They can afford to have a thicker consistency because you won't need to apply make-up over the top.

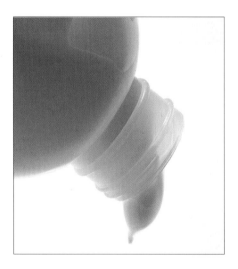

Above: Put some zing into your skin-care regime with a refreshing toner or astringent.

Above: Creamy cleansers should be a top priority for drier complexions, as they cleanse and nourish at the same time.

Right: Before you tailormake a skin-care regime for yourself, you need to know the key benefits of each product.

THE FRESH APPROACH TO OILY SKIN

This skin-type usually has open pores and an oily surface, with a tendency towards pimples, blackheads and a sallow appearance. This is due to the over-production of the oily substance called sebum by the oil glands in the lower layers of the skin. Unfortunately, this skin-type is the one most prone to acne. The good news is that this oiliness will make your skin stay younger-looking for longer – so there are some benefits!

SPECIAL CARE FOR YOUR SKIN

It's important not to treat oily skin too harshly, although this can be tempting when you're faced with a fresh outbreak of pimples. Over-enthusiastic treatment can encourage the oil glands to produce even more sebum, whilst it will leave the surface layers dry and dehydrated.

The best care way to care for oily skin is to use products that gently cleanse away oils from the surface and unblock pores, without drying out and damaging it. The visible part of your skin actually needs water, not oil, to stay soft and supple.

ACNE ALERT

Anyone who has acne knows what a distressing condition it is. It usually appears in our lives at the one time when we're already feeling insecure – adolescence. As well as being a problem that runs in families, it's thought to be triggered by a change in hormones, which results in more sebum being produced by your skin. It can also be aggravated by stress, poor lifestyle and poor skin-care.

Careful skin-care will help keep acne under control. Avoid picking at pimples, as this can lead to scarring. Try over-the-counter blemish treatments. Today's formulations contain ingredients that are very successful at treating this problem. Products containing tea tree oil can be very effective. If these aren't successful, consult your doctor who may be able to provide treatment, or can refer you to a dermatologist.

1 Even though the remainder of your face is prone to oiliness, always remember that the skin around your eyes is very delicate, so don't drag at it when removing your eye make-up. Soak a cottonwool (cotton) pad with a non-oily remover and hold over your eyes for a few seconds to give it time to dissolve the make-up. Then lightly stroke away the mascara and make-up from the eyelids, and your upper and lower lashes.

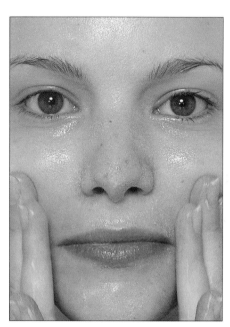

2 Lather up with a gentle foaming facial wash. This is a better choice than ordinary soap, as it won't strip away moisture from your skin, but it will remove grime, dirt and oil. Massage gently over damp skin with your fingertips, then rinse away the soapy suds with lots of warm water.

3 Soak a cottonwool (cotton) ball with a refreshing astringent lotion. Sweep it over your skin to refresh and cool it. This liquid should not irritate or sting your skin – if it does, swap to a product with a gentler formulation or water your existing one down with some distilled water from the pharmacist. Continue until the cottonwool (cotton) comes up completely clean.

4 Even oily skins need moisturizer, because a moisturizer helps seal water into the top layers to keep the skin soft and supple. However, don't load the skin down with a very heavy formulation. Instead, choose a light, watery fluid as this will be enough for you.

Below: Boosting your skin's moisture levels and controlling excess oiliness will ensure a beautifully clear complexion.

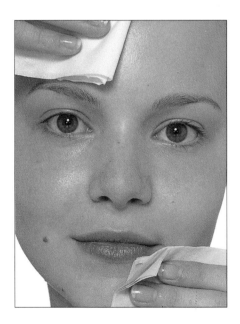

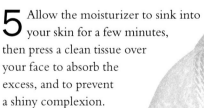

5 Allow the moisturizer to sink into your skin for a few minutes, then press a clean tissue over your face to absorb the excess, and to prevent a shiny complexion.

NOURISHING CARE FOR DRY SKIN

If your skin tends to feel one size too small, it's a fair bet you've got a dry complexion. It's caused by too little sebum in the lower levels of skin, and too little moisture in the upper levels. At its best, it can feel tight and itchy after washing. At its worse it can be flaky, with little patches of dandruff in your eyebrows, and a tendency to premature ageing with the emergence of fine lines and wrinkles. It requires soothing care to look its best.

SPECIAL CARE FOR YOUR SKIN

The condition of dry skin can be aggravated by over-use of soap, detergents and toners. It is also affected by exposure to hot sun, cold winds and central heating. Opt for the gentle approach, concentrating on boosting the skin's moisture level to plump out fine lines and make it soft and supple.

Below: Nourish dry skin to keep it as soft and supple as possible.

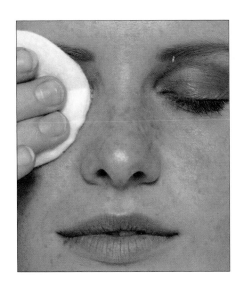  

1 Pour a little oil-based eye make-up remover onto a cottonwool (cotton) pad and sweep it over the eye area. This oily product will also help soothe away dryness in the delicate eye area, but a little goes a long way. If you overload the skin here with an oily product it can cause puffiness and irritation.

2 Clean up stubborn flecks with a cotton bud (swab) dipped in the eye make-up remover. Be careful not to get the remover in your eyes but work as closely as you can to the eyelashes to remove all signs of make-up.

3 Choose a creamy cleanser which will melt away dirt and make-up from the surface of your skin. It's essential to ensure your skin is really clean. Leave the cleanser on for a few moments for it to work, before sweeping it away with a cottonwool (cotton) pad. Use gentle upward movements to prevent stretching the skin and encouraging lines.

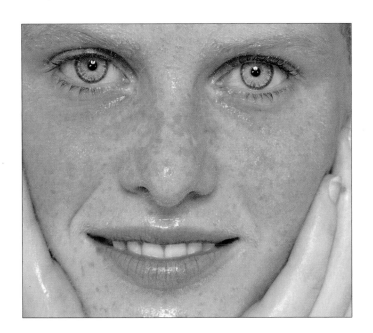 

4 One of the main complaints from women with dry skin is that they miss the feeling of water on their skin. However, you can splash your face with cool water to remove excess cleanser and to refresh your skin. This will also help boost the circulation, which means a brighter complexion.

5 This is the most important step of all for dry skins - a nourishing cream to seal moisture into the upper levels of your skin. Opt for a thick cream, rather than a runny lotion, as this contains more oil than water, and will help seal in more moisture. Give the moisturizer a few minutes to sink into your skin before applying make-up.

BALANCED CARE FOR COMBINATION SKIN

Combination skin needs careful care because it has a blend of oily and dry patches. The centre panel, or T-zone, across the forehead and down the nose and chin tends to be oily, and needs to be treated like oily skin. However, the other areas are prone to dryness and flakiness due to lack of moisture, and need to be treated like dry skin. Having said this, some combination skins don't follow the T-zone pattern and can have patches of dry and oily skin in other arrangements. If you're unsure of your skin's oily and dry areas, press a tissue to your face an hour after washing it. Any greasy patches on the tissue signify oily areas.

SPECIAL CARE FOR YOUR SKIN

Because your skin-type has a combination of dry and oily patches, you need a twin approach to skin-care. Treating your entire complexion like oily skin will leave the dry areas even drier and tighter than before. In the same way, treating it only like dry skin can provoke excess oiliness and even an outbreak of blemishes. This means you need to deal with the different areas of skin individually with products to suit. This isn't as complicated and difficult as it sounds, and the result will be a softer, smoother and clearer complexion than before!

Left: A twin approach to skin-care will double the benefits for combination skin, and it needn't be terribly time-consuming.

1 Choose an oil-based eye make-up remover to clear away every trace of eye make-up from this delicate area which is prone to dryness. Use a cotton bud (swab) to remove any stubborn traces. Splash with cool water afterwards to rinse away any excess oil.

2 Use a foaming facial wash in the morning to cleanse your skin. This will ensure the oily areas are clean, and that the pores on your nose are kept clear to prevent blackheads and blemishes. Massage a little onto damp skin, concentrating on the oily areas. Leave for a few seconds to dissolve the dirt, then splash with cool water to remove the cleanser.

3 In the evening, switch to a cream cleanser, to ensure the dry areas of skin are kept clean and soothed on a daily basis. This will give you a balance between excess oiliness or excess dryness in your complexion. Massage well into your skin, concentrating on the drier areas, then gently remove with cotton-wool (cotton) pads.

4 To freshen your skin, you need to buy two different strengths of toners to deal with the differing areas of skin. Choose a stronger astringent for the oily areas, and a mild skin freshener for the drier ones. This isn't as expensive as you think, because you'll only need to use a little of each. Sweep over your skin with cottonwool (cotton) pads.

5 Smooth moisturizer onto your entire skin, concentrating on the drier areas. Then blot off any excess from the oily areas with a tissue. This will give all your skin the nourishment it needs.

MAINTAINING NORMAL SKIN

This is the perfect, balanced skin-type! It has a healthy glow, with a fine texture and no open pores. It rarely develops spots or shiny areas. In fact, it's quite rare to find a normal skin, especially as all skins tend to become slightly drier as you get older.

SPECIAL CARE FOR YOUR SKIN

Your main concern is to keep normal skin functioning well, and as a result of this let it continue the good job it's already doing! It naturally has a good balance of oil and moisture levels. Your routine should include gently cleansing your skin to ensure surface grime and stale make-up are removed, and to prevent a build-up of sebum. Then you should boost moisture levels with moisturizer, to protect and pamper your skin.

1 Eye make-up should always be removed carefully. Going to bed with mascara on can lead to sore, puffy eyes. Applying new make-up on the top of stale make-up is positively unhygienic, too! Choose your product according to whether you're wearing ordinary or waterproof mascara.

2 Splash your face with water, then massage in a gentle facial wash and work it up to a lather for about 30 seconds. Take the opportunity to lightly massage your skin, as this will boost the supply of blood to the surface of your skin – which means a rosier complexion.

3 Rinse away with clear water until every soapy trace has been removed from your skin. Then pat your face with a soft towel to absorb residual water from the surface of your skin. Don't rub at your skin, especially around the eyes, as this can encourage wrinkling.

4 Cool your skin with a freshening toner. Again, avoid the delicate eye area as this can become more prone to dryness.

5 Smooth your skin with moisturizing lotion. Dot onto your face, then massage in with your fingertips using light upwards strokes. This will leave a protective film on the skin, allowing make-up to be easily applied and ensuring there's a balanced moisture content.

Below: Follow a regular skin-care regime to
keep normal skin as fresh as a daisy!

SOOTHING CARE FOR SENSITIVE SKIN

Sensitive skin is usually quite fine in texture, with a tendency to be rosier than usual. Easily irritated by products and external factors, it's also prone to redness and allergy, and may have fine broken veins across the cheeks and nose. There are varying levels of sensitivity. If you feel you can't use any products on your skin without irritating it, cleanse with whole milk and moisturize with a solution of glycerin and rosewater. These should soothe it.

SPECIAL CARE FOR YOUR SKIN

Your skin needs extra-gentle products to keep it healthy. Choose from hypo-allergenic ranges that are specially formulated to protect sensitive skin. They're screened for common irritants, such as fragrance, that can cause dryness, itchiness or even an allergic reaction.

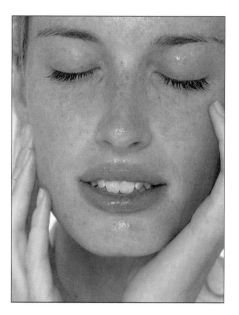

2 Steer clear of facial washes and soaps on your skin, as these are likely to strip your skin of oil and moisture which can increase its sensitivity even more. So, instead, choose a light, hypo-allergenic cleansing lotion.

3 Even the mildest skin freshener can break down the natural protection your delicate skin needs against the elements. So freshen it by simply splashing with a warm water instead. This will also remove the final traces of cleanser and eye make-up remover from your skin.

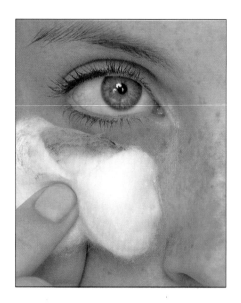

1 Make sure the make-up you use is hypo-allergenic, too, and remove it thoroughly. First use a soothing eye make-up remover. Apply with a cotton-wool (cotton) ball, then remove every last trace with a clean cotton bud (swab).

4 Lightly pat your face dry with a soft towel, taking care not to rub the skin as this could irritate it. (Right)

Below: Careful skin-care will take the sting out of sensitive skin.

5 It's essential to keep your skin well moisturized to strengthen it and provide a barrier against irritants that can lead to sensitivity. Dryness can make sensitive skin even more uncomfortable and irritated, so don't forget to choose an unperfumed moisturizer.

MIRACULOUS MASKS

If there's one skin-care item that can work immediate miracles, it's a face mask! But, like any other skin-care product, you can't just reach for the first one and hope for the best. You should choose carefully to pick the perfect product for you.

MASK IT!

Choose from the wonderful selection of face masks on the market.

Moisturizing masks

These are ideal for dry complexions as they'll boost the moisture levels of your skin. This means they can help banish dry patches, flakiness and even fine lines. They work quickly like an intensive moisturizer, and are usually left on the skin for 5-10 minutes before being removed with a tissue. The slight residue left on your skin will continue to work until you next cleanse your skin. They're a great treat, particularly after sunbathing, or when your skin feels "tight".

Clay and mud masks

These are great for oily skins as they'll absorb excess grease and impurities from your skin, leaving it looking cleaner and fresher. They're an ideal way to "shrink" open pores, blot out shininess and clear away troublesome blemishes. They dry on your skin over a period of 5-15 minutes, then you simply wash them away with warm water, rinsing dead skin cells, dirt and grime away at the same time. They're a great pick-me-up for skin.

Exfoliating masks

Masks with a light exfoliating action can keep your skin in tip-top condition. Even normal skins sometimes suffer from the build-up of dead skin cells, which can create a dull look and lead to future problems such as blackheads. Masks that cleanse and exfoliate are the perfect solution. They smooth on like a clay mask, and are left to dry. When you rinse them away, their tiny abrasive particles slough away the skin's surface debris.

Above: Clay and mud masks: they dry on your skin over a period of 5-15 minutes.

> **TIP**
> If you have combination skin, take this tip from the beauty salons and use two masks – one suitable for oily skin and one for dry skin. Just apply each one to the relevant area that needs it.

Peel-off masks

These are great for all skin-types, and fun to use. You smooth on the gel, leave it to dry, then peel it away. The light formulation will help refresh oily areas, by clearing clogged pores, as well as lightly nourishing drier skins.

Gel masks

These are suitable for sensitive skins, as well as oily complexions, as they have a wonderfully soothing and cooling effect. You simply apply the gel, lie back, then tissue off the excess after 5-10 minutes. They're wonderful after too much sun, or when your skin feels irritated.

POINTS TO REMEMBER

● Your skin can change with the seasons. For instance, skin that becomes oily in the hot summer months can become drier in winter and in central heating. So take your skin's own particular quirks into account when choosing your mask.

● Cleanse your face before applying your chosen mask. Afterwards, rinse with warm water, then apply moisturizer.

● Most masks should be left on the skin for between 3-10 minutes. For the best results, read the instructions carefully.

FACIAL SCRUBS – GRAINS OF TRUTH

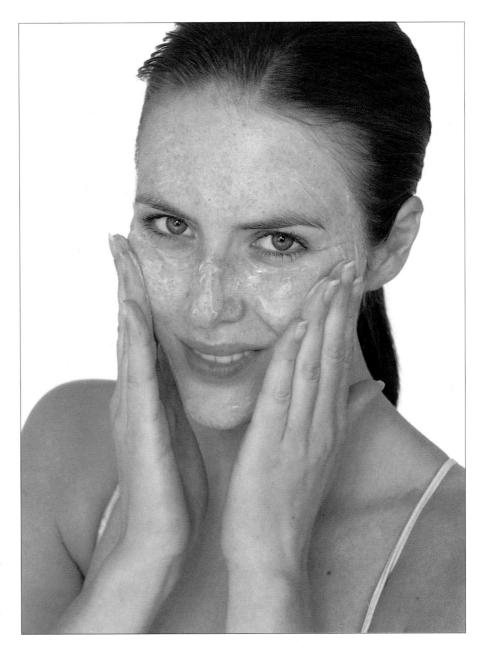

Brighten up your complexion in an instant with this skin-care treat! If you don't include a facial scrub in your weekly skin-care regime, then you've been missing out! Technically known as exfoliation, it's a simple method that whisks away dead surface cells from the top of your skin, revealing the plumper, younger ones underneath. It also encourages your skin to speed up cell production, which means that the cells that reach the surface are younger and better-looking. The result is, a brighter, smoother complexion - no matter what your age.

ACTION TACTICS

Use an exfoliater on dry or normal skin once or twice a week. Oily or combination skins can be exfoliated every other day. As a rule, avoid this treatment on sensitive skin, or if you have bad acne. However, you can gently exfoliate pimple-prone skin once a week to help keep pores clear and prevent break-outs.

GETTING TO THE NITTY-GRITTY

● Apply a blob of facial scrub cream to damp skin, massage gently, then rinse away with lots of cool water. Opt for an exfoliater that contains gentler, rounded beads, rather than scratchy ones like crushed kernels.
● Try a mini exfoliating pad, lathering up with soap or facial wash.

Above: Get your skin glowing with a quick and easy facial treat.
Left: Instead of using a facial scrub, gently massage your skin with a soft flannel, facial brush, or old, clean shaving brush.

TIP
Whichever method of exfoliation you use, avoid the delicate eye area. This is because the skin is very fine here and can be easily irritated.

DELICATE CARE FOR EYES

The fine skin around your eyes is the first to show the signs of ageing, as well as dark circles and puffiness. Don't be tempted to deal with the problem by slapping on heavy oils and moisturizers - your eyes will benefit more from specially designed eye creams and gels. The delicate skin around your eyes needs extra special care because it's thinner than the skin on the rest of your face, so it's less able to hold in moisture. There are also fewer oil glands in this area, which adds to the potential dryness, and there's no fatty layer underneath the skin to act as a shock absorber. The result is that this skin quickly loses its elasticity.

Below: Moisturizing the very delicate skin surrounding the eyes calls for special products.

CHOOSING AN EYE TREATMENT

Face creams and oils are too heavy for the eye area. They can block tear ducts, causing puffiness, so you should choose a specific eye treatment that won't aggravate your skin. There are hundreds of products to choose from. Gel-based ones are great for young or oily skins, and are refreshing to use. However, most women find light eye creams and balms more suitable.

Use a tiny amount of the eye treatment, as you don't want to overload this area. It's better to apply it regularly in small quantities than apply lots only occasionally. Apply with your ring finger, as this is the weakest one on your hand and won't stretch the delicate skin. This will help keep your skin more supple, and prevent premature wrinkling in this area.

PREVENTING PUFFY EYES

This is one of the most common beauty problems. These ideas can help:
● Gently tap your skin with your ring finger when you're applying eye cream to encourage the excess fluid to drain away.
● Store creams in the refrigerator, as the coldness will also help reduce puffiness.
● Place strips of grated potato under your eyes to help reduce swelling. Strawberries and cucumber can also help.
● Fill a small bowl with iced water or ice-cold milk. Soak a cottonwool (cotton) pad with the liquid and lie down with the dampened pads over your eyes. Replace the pads as soon as they become warm. Continue for 15 minutes. As well as reducing puffiness, this treatment will brighten the whites of your eyes.

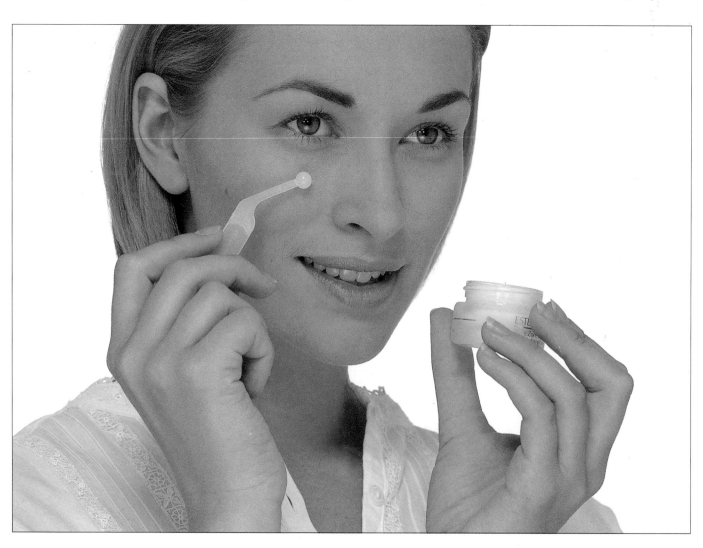

GOOD NIGHT CREAMS

Going to bed with night cream on your face can benefit your skin while you sleep. The main difference between night creams and ordinary daily moisturizers is that most night creams have added ingredients such as vitamins and anti-ageing components. They can be thicker and more intensive than day creams because you don't need to wear make-up on top of them.

Your skin's cell renewal is more active during the night, and night creams are designed to make the most of these hours. Using a night cream gives your skin the chance to repair the daily wear and tear caused by pollution, make-up and ultra-violet light.

Above: Applying night cream before bed means waking up to a softer complexion.
Left: Dry areas, like cheeks, will absorb the extra moisture a night cream can give.

WHO NEEDS NIGHT CREAMS?

While very young skins don't really need the extra nourishing properties of night creams, most women will benefit from using one. Dry and very dry skins respond particularly well. You don't have to choose very rich formulations, as there are lighter alternatives that contain the same special ingredients. Choose the formulation on the basis of how dry your skin is – it shouldn't feel overloaded.

Applying night cream to slightly damp skin can really boost its performance, as this seals in extra moisture – which means softer, smoother skin in the morning.

BE A FRUITY BEAUTY

Since their launch a couple of years ago, skin-care products that contain alpha-hydroxy acids (AHAs) have grown in popularity. They've become the biggest skin-care invention of the 1990s, and their success looks set to continue. Many women find they dramatically improve the condition and look of their skins.

AHA KNOW-HOW

Alpha-hydroxy acids, also commonly known as fruit acids, are found in natural products. These include citric acid from citrus fruit; lactic acid from sour milk; tartaric acid from wine, and malic acid from apples and other fruits. Incorporated in small amounts, AHAs have recently become a key ingredient in specialized skin-care products.

They work by breaking down the protein bonds that hold together the dead cells on the surface of your skin. They then lift them away and reveal the brighter, plumper cells underneath. This gentle process cleans and clears blocked pores, improves your skin-tone and softens the look of fine lines. Basically, they're the ideal solution to most minor skin-care problems. You should start to see results within a couple of weeks. Many women report that they see an improvement after only a few days.

Without even realizing it, women have used AHAs for centuries and have reaped the benefits on their skins. For example Cleopatra is said to have bathed in asses' sour milk and ladies of the French court applied wine to their faces to keep their skin smooth, supple and blemish free – both these ancient beauty aids are now known to contain AHAs.

AHA products are best used under your ordinary everyday moisturizer as a treatment cream. You should avoid applying them to the delicate eye and lip areas. If you have very sensitive skin, you may find they're not suitable for you, but some women experience a slight tingling sensation at first anyway, as the product gets to work.

The great news is that AHA products are now becoming more affordable, and not just the preserve of more expensive skin-care companies. Many mid-market companies are including the benefits of AHAs in their products, so everyone can give their skin the high-tech treatment it deserves. You can also find AHA products for the hands and body, so you can reap the benefits from top to toe.

Above: AHAs (otherwise known as fruit acids) are an effective way to put the zing back into your skin. In fact, there's nothing new about AHAs – by bathing in asses' milk Cleopatra was absorbing AHAs into her skin.

SPECIAL SKIN TREATMENTS

You'd be forgiven for thinking you need a PhD in chemistry to choose a skin treatment these days! As well as basic moisturizers, there are a whole host of special treatments, serums and gels that are designed to treat specific problems.

THE KEY TREATMENTS

You'll find that special skin treatments come in all shapes and sizes, and in various formulations.

Serums and gels

These have an ultra-light formulation, a non-greasy texture and a high concentration of active ingredients. They're not usually designed to be used on their own, except on oily skins. They're generally applied under a moisturizer to enhance its benefits and boost the anti-ageing process.

Above: Good things come in small packages – highly effective ingredients often come in tiny ampules.

Ampule treatments

These are very concentrated active ingredients contained in sealed glass phials or ampules, to ensure that they're very fresh. Typical extracts include herbs, wheat germ, vitamins and collagen – used for their intensive and fast-acting results. Vitamin E is another great skin saver. Break open a capsule and smooth the oil onto your face for an immediate skin treat.

Liposome creams

Liposomes are tiny spheres within the cream which contain and carry special ingredients into the skin. Their shells break down once they're absorbed into the upper layers of your skin, releasing the active ingredients.

Above: Just a few drops of a special skin serum will work wonders on your skin.

Below: Choose a cream that contains specialized ingredients to improve your skin.

Skin-firmers

You can lift your skin instantly with creams that are designed to tighten, firm and smooth. They work by forming an ultra-fine film on the skin, which tightens your complexion and reduces the appearance of fine lines. The effects last for a few hours, and make-up can easily be applied on top. These products are a wonderful treat for a special night out or when you're feeling particularly tired.

Skin energizers

These are creams that contain special ingredients designed to speed up the natural production and repair of skin cells. As well as producing a fresher, younger-looking skin, this is also thought to help combat the signs of ageing.

TRY A FABULOUS FACIAL

For deep-down cleansing and a definite improvement in skin-tone, try an at-home facial. Just once a month will make a noticeable difference to your complexion. Follow these steps to re-create the benefits of the beauty salon in the comfort and privacy of your own home.

1 Smooth your skin with cleansing cream. Leave on for 1-2 minutes to give it time to dissolve grime, oils and stale make-up. Then gently smooth away with cottonwool (cotton).

2 Dampen your skin with warm water. Then, gently massage with a blob of facial scrub, avoiding the delicate eye area. This will loosen dead surface skin cells, and leave your skin softer and smoother. It will also prepare your complexion for the beneficial treatments to come. Rinse away with warm water.

3 Fill a bowl or wash basin with a kettleful of boiling water. Then lean over the top, capturing the steam with a towel placed over your head. Stay there for 5 minutes, to allow the steam to warm and soften your skin. If you have any blackheads, you can try to gently remove them with tissue-covered fingers after this treatment. If you suffer from very sensitive skin, or are prone to broken veins, you should avoid this step.

4 Smooth on a face mask. Choose a clay-based one if you have oily skin, or a moisturizing one if you have dry or normal skin. Leave on for 5 minutes, or for as long as specified by the instructions on the product.

5 Rinse away the face mask with warm water. Finish off with a few splashes of cool water to close your pores and freshen your skin, then pat dry with a towel.

6 Soak a cottonwool (cotton) pad with a skin toner lotion, and smooth over oily areas, such as the nose, chin and forehead.

7 Dot your skin with moisturizer and smooth in. Take the opportunity to massage your skin, as this encourages a brighter complexion and can help reduce puffiness.

8 Smooth your undereye areas with a soothing eye cream to reduce fine lines and wrinkles, and make the skin ultra-soft.

EATING FOR BEAUTIFUL SKIN

While lotions and potions can improve your skin from the outside, a healthy diet works from the inside out. A nutritious, balanced diet isn't only a delicious way to eat – it can work wonders for your skin.

YOU ARE WHAT YOU EAT

A diet for a healthy body is the same one as for a healthy, clear complexion. That is, one that contains lots of fresh fruit and vegetables, is high in fibre, low in fat, and low in added sugar and salt. This should provide your body and your skin with all the vitamins and minerals needed to function at their very best.

Healthy skin checklist

These are the essentials your body needs to keep your skin in tip-top condition.
1 The most essential element is water. Although there's water in the foods you eat, you should drink at least two litres (quarts) of water a day to keep your body healthy and your skin clear.

Below: A fresh and fruity diet will keep your complexion looking good.

2 Cellulose carbohydrates, better known as fibre foods, have another less direct effect on the skin. Their action in keeping you regular can help to give you a brighter, clearer complexion.
3 Vitamin A is essential for growth and repair of certain skin tissues. Lack of it causes dryness, itching and loss of skin elasticity. It's found in foods such as carrots, spinach, broccoli and apricots.
4 Vitamin C is needed for collagen production, to help keep your skin firm. It's found in foods such as strawberries, citrus fruits, cabbage, tomatoes and watercress.
5 Vitamin E is an antioxidant vitamin that neutralizes free radicals – highly reactive molecules that can cause ageing. It occurs in foods such as almonds, hazelnuts and wheat germ.
6 Zinc works with vitamin A in the making of collagen and elastin, the fibres that give your skin its strength, elasticity and firmness.

DIET Q & A

A healthy diet and a beautiful complexion go hand in hand together. Check you know the facts.

1 Yo-yo dieting

Q *"Is it true that constantly losing and gaining weight can have a bad effect on your skin?"*

A Yes. Eating too much and becoming overweight thickens the layer of fat under your skin and consequently stretches it. Crash dieting can then result in your skin collapsing, leading to the appearance of lines and wrinkles. What's more, a crash diet will deprive your skin and body of the essential nutrients they need to stay healthy and look good. If you need to lose weight, do it slowly, sensibly and steadily, to give your skin time to acclimatize. It's always advisable to consult your doctor before starting any weight loss programme.

2 Daily diet

Q *"What would be a good typical day's diet for a clearer complexion?"*

A One that follows the rules already outlined. For example, here's a typical day you could follow.
Breakfast: A glass of unsweetened fruit juice; bowl of unsweetened muesli (whole grain cereal), topped with a chopped banana and semi-skimmed (1 per cent or skim) milk; two slices of wholewheat toast with a scraping of low-fat spread.
Lunch: Baked potato, filled with low-fat cottage cheese and plenty of fresh, raw salad; one low-fat yogurt, any flavour.
Evening meal: Grilled fish or chicken, with boiled brown rice, and plenty of steamed vegetables. Fresh fruit salad, topped with natural yogurt and nuts.

3 On the spot

Q *"Does chocolate cause pimples?"*

A There isn't any scientific evidence that links eating chocolate to having breakouts, but as a healthy low-fat, high-fibre diet is known to be good for skin, keep snacks such as chocolate to a minimum and eat them only as an occasional treat.

Below: It's clearly obvious, drinking plenty of
water during the day helps purify your body
– which means a fresher, firmer skin.

10 WAYS TO BEAT WRINKLES

Fine lines and wrinkles aren't inevitable. In fact, skin experts believe that most skin damage can be prevented with a little know-how and some special care. Here are the 10 main points to bear in mind, no matter what your age.

1 Protect your skin from the sun

The single biggest cause of skin ageing is sunlight. You should use a sunscreen every single day of the year. This will help prevent your skin from becoming prematurely aged, as well as guard against burning. The ageing rays of the sun are as prevalent in the cold winter months as in the hot summer ones, so it's a daily safeguard you should take.

2 Stop smoking

Cigarette smoke speeds up the ageing process because it strips your skin of oxygen and slows down the rate at which new cells are regenerated. It's responsible for giving the skin a grey, sluggish look,

and can cause fine lines around the mouth because heavy smokers tend to be constantly pursing their lips to draw on a cigarette.

3 Deep cleanse

Many older women don't cleanse their skin as thoroughly as they should, believing this can lead to dryness and lines. However, it's essential to ensure your skin is clear of dead skin cells, dirt and make-up to give it a youthful, fresh glow.

You don't have to use harsh products to do this – a creamy cleanser removed with cottonwool (cotton) is a good option for most women. If your skin is very dry, try massaging it with an oily cleanser. Leave it on your skin for a few minutes, then rinse away the excess with warm water.

4 Deep moisturize

As well as a daily moisturizer, you can also boost the water levels of your skin on a weekly basis. You can either use a nourishing face mask, or apply a thick layer of your usual moisturizer or night cream. Whichever you choose, leave it on the skin for 5-10 minutes, then remove the excess with tissues. Apply to damp skin for greater effect.

5 Boost the circulation

Buy a gentle facial scrub or exfoliater, and use once a week to keep the surface of your skin soft and smooth. This will also increase the blood flow to the top layers of skin, giving it a rosy glow and help encourage cell renewal. Alternatively, you can get the same effect by lathering up a facial wash on your skin using a clean shaving brush.

6 Disguise lines

Existing lines can be minimized to the naked eye by opting for the latest light-reflecting foundations, concealers and powders. These contain luminescent particles to bounce light away from your skin, making lines less noticeable and giving your skin a wonderful luminosity.

7 Pamper regularly

As well as a regular skin-care regime, remember to treat your skin occasionally to special treatments such as facials, serums and anti-ageing creams. As well as improving the look of your skin, they'll encourage you to give it extra care on a regular basis.

8 Be weather vain

Extremes of cold and hot weather can strip your skin of essential moisture, leaving it dry and more prone to damage. Central heating can have the same effect. For this reason, ensure you moisturize regularly, changing your products according to the seasons.

For instance, you may need a more oily product in the winter, which will keep the cold out and won't freeze on the skin's surface. In hot weather, lighter formulations are more comfortable on the skin, and you can boost their activity by using a few drops of special treatment serum underneath.

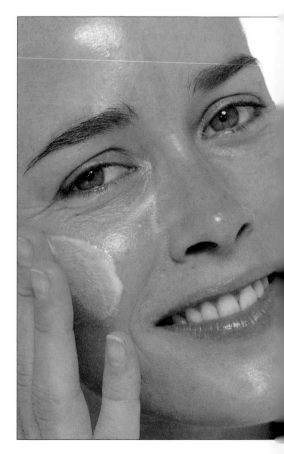

9 Be gentle

Be careful you don't drag at your skin when applying skin-care products or make-up. The skin around your eyes is particularly vulnerable to showing the signs of ageing. A heavy touch can cause the skin to stretch and go crepey. So, make sure you always use a light touch instead, and whenever you can, take your strokes upwards, rather than drag the skin down. Also, avoid any products that make your skin itch, sting or feel sensitive. If any product causes this sort of reaction, stop using it at once, and switch to a gentler formulation.

10 Clever make-up

Skin-care benefits aren't just confined to skin-care products these days. In fact, many make-up products now contain UV filters and skin-nourishing ingredients to treat your skin as well as superficially improve it's appearance. So investigate the latest products – it's well worth making use of them for 24-hour day benefits.

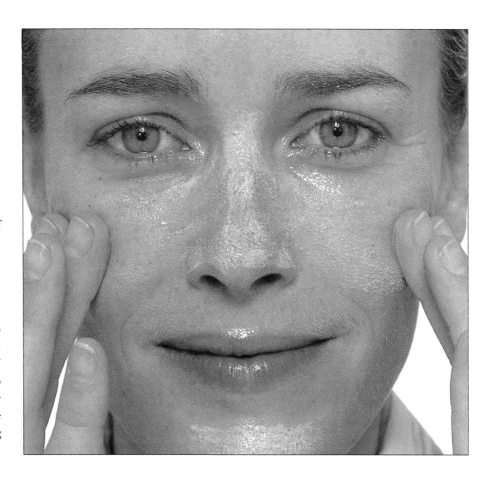

This page (above): Wake up to the benefits of special skin-care treatments.
This page (left): Relax and enjoy a beneficial facial!

Opposite page (left): You won't believe the difference regular cleansing can make.
Opposite page (right): Protect and survive with a good moisturizer.

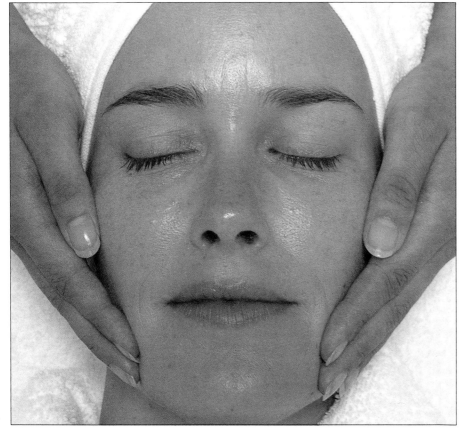

YOUR TOP 20 SKIN-CARE QUESTIONS ANSWERED

1 Night watch

Q *"My dry skin needs night cream, but I seem to lose most of it onto my pillow. Any solutions?"*

A Put a little night cream into the palm of your hand, then gently rub your hands together. The heat created will help liquefy the cream and make it more easily absorbed. Gently massage it into your skin, and you'll find it sinks in better. Another method is to place the cream in a teaspoon, and heat gently over a low gas flame on the cooker until just warm, before applying as usual. It sounds strange, but really works!

Above: The soft touch of a sponge is a cheap – and effective – option to facial scrub.

2 Polished perfection

Q *"I spend a fortune on skin-care products, but resent paying for an exfoliater. Are there any alternatives?"*

A Yes, here's a good, cheap alternative to facial scrubs! After washing your skin, gently massage with a soft facecloth or natural sponge to ease away the dead surface skin cells which can give your complexion a muddy look. Make sure you avoid ones with scratchy surfaces as they'll be too harsh for your skin. If you have dry skin, massage a little cream cleanser onto damp skin, then rub over the top with

your flannel. Rinse afterwards, then apply moisturizer in the normal way. However, it is essential to wash the facecloth after every couple of uses, and to hang it up to dry in between to prevent the build-up of bacteria.

3 Lip tricks

Q *"How can I stop my lips getting so chapped and flaky in winter?"*

A This three-step action plan will help.
a) Massage dry lips with a generous dollop of petroleum jelly. Allow it to get to work for a couple of minutes to soften your skin. Then, gently rub your lips with a warm, damp facecloth. As the petroleum jelly is removed, the flakes of skin will come with it!
b) Smooth your lips morning and night with a lip balm.
c) Switch to a moisturizing lipstick to prevent your lips from drying out during the daytime.

4 Red nose day

Q *"It's so embarrassing! My nose looks really red in the winter. What's the best way to cover it?"*

A Try smoothing a little green foundation or concealer over the red area before applying your normal foundation and powder. Although it sounds strange, the green works by cancelling out the redness – leaving your skin looking a normal shade again.

5 Winter sun

Q *"Someone told me you should still wear a sunscreen in winter. Is this true?"*

A Yes, if you want to guard against the signs of ageing! Exposure to sunlight is thought to be the main cause of wrinkling, and the ultraviolet A rays that are responsible for this process are around every single day of the year. You don't, however, need to use a suntan lotion – just choose one of the many moisturizers that contain sunscreens.

6 Lighten up

Q *"My skin feels as though it needs a richer cream in the winter months, but I find most of them too heavy. What can you suggest?"*

A Just choose the level of moisturizer that feels right for you. Just because a moisturizer is heavier, it doesn't necessarily mean it's more effective. You can help seal in extra moisture to your skin by spritzing your complexion with water before

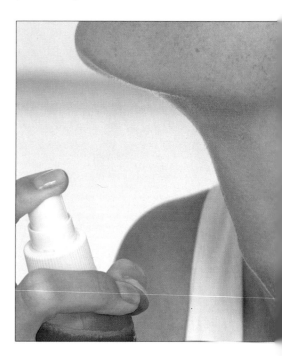

Above: Puttin' on the spritz – boost the moisture in your skin.

applying it. Also, choose a nourishing foundation or tinted moisturizer to ensure your skin stays smooth and soft all day long. You can help counteract the drying effects of central heating by placing a bowl of water near the radiators to replenish moisture levels in the air.

7 Water factor

Q *"I like the feeling of water on my face, but I find soap too drying. Should I switch to a cream cleanser instead?"*

A If you have dry skin, it's generally better to use a creamy cleanser, which you

Left: Cream cleanser will get dry skin deep-down clean.

apply with your fingertips and remove with cottonwool (cotton) or soft tissues. This is because it will prevent too much moisture from being lost from the surface of your skin. However, normal and oily skins can still happily use water – but switch to a facial wash or wash-off cleanser instead. They're specially formulated to be non-drying, while still getting your face clean – and you can splash with water as much as you like!

8 Age spots

Q *"I've noticed 'liver spots' appearing on the back of my hands. How are they caused – and how can I get rid of them?"*

A Many people find these light-to-dark brown patches appearing on the back of their hands as they grow older. They can also appear on other areas, such as the forehead and temples. They're caused by an uneven production of the tanning pigment called melanin in the skin. This can be caused by excess sun exposure, or merely highlighted by it.

You can use a cream containing an ingredient called hydroquinone, which works by penetrating the skin tissue to "dissolve" the melanin. Within six to eight weeks, your skin should be back to normal. However, you must ensure you use a safe level of hydroquinone – the recommended amount in a cream is a mere two per cent. Using a sunscreen on your hands on a daily basis can prevent these patches from appearing again.

9 Sensitive issue

Q *"Why does my skin feel more sensitive in winter than summer?"*

A Eighty per cent of women claim to have sensitive skin – which tingles, itches and is prone to dryness. It can be aggravated by harsh winter weather, such as the winds and cold, because this breaks down the natural oily layer which protects your skin. Milder summer weather doesn't tend to be so hard on the skin. The best way to cope is to moisturize regularly with a hypo-allergenic cream that is specially formulated for sensitive skin.

10 Pregnant pause

Q *"I'm pregnant and have developed patches of darker colour on my face, particularly under my eyes and around my mouth. What causes this?"*

A This is called chloasma, or "the mask of pregnancy". It's triggered by a change in hormones at this time, and is made more obvious by sunbathing. Cover up under the sun and wear a sunblock to prevent the patches from becoming denser. It usually fades within a few months of having your baby. Chloasma can also be triggered by birth-control pills, but disappears once you stop taking them.

11 On the spot

Q *I suffer from oily skin, but find blemish creams too drying. What can you suggest?*

A Many women have skin that has dry patches as well as blemishes. The solution is to choose an antibacterial cream that will kill off the cause of your blemishes, while soothing the skin around them. This means you won't be left with dry patches of skin as well as blemishes.

12 Treatment sprays

Q *"I find body lotions too hot and sticky to wear after bathing. Is there anything else I can try?"*

A There's a lovely new trend for body treatment sprays, which combine the moisturizing and toning properties of a body care product with the fragrance of a traditional perfume. This means they'll make you smell beautifully fresh as well as lightly moisturizing your skin. Many of the large perfume companies now offer a choice of these products.

13 The throat vote

Q *"The skin on my neck looks grey and dull. Are there any special treats to use?"*

A Necks can quickly show the signs of ageing. This is mainly due to the fact that they have a lack of sebaceous glands. Using a creamy cleanser can help. Massage in, leave to dissolve dirt, and then remove with cottonwool (cotton) pads. Dull grey skin will benefit from regular exfoliation - scrub briskly with a face cloth or soft shaving brush. Grey lines on neck and throat can be bleached away by smoothing plain yogurt over clean skin. Leave on for about half an hour, then rinse away thoroughly with warm water. Boost softness by smoothing on moisturizer. There's no need for a specialized throat cream – your ordinary one will do.

14 Beautiful back

Q *"How can I get rid of the pimples on my back and bottom?"*

A Because backs are covered up, and hard to reach, they're prone to breakouts. Keep yours blemish-free by exfoliating daily with a loofah or body brush to remove dry, flaking skin and superficial blemishes. For more stubborn pimples, try a clay mask to draw out deep-seated impurities. Smooth onto broken-out areas, leave until dry, then rinse away with lots of warm water.

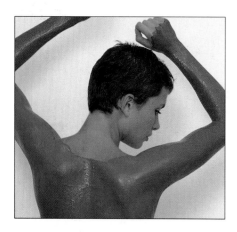

Above: Back to basics with a clay mask for the body.

15 Mole watch

Q *"I understand you need to keep an eye on moles on your skin to guard against the risk of skin cancer. But what exactly should I be looking for?"*

A Moles are clumps of clustered pigment cells that are nearly always darker than freckles. All changes in existing moles should be checked by your doctor. Any that cause concern will be removed and sent off for analysis. You should also check moles yourself once a month. Try the following A.B.C.D. Code: check for A (asymmetry); B (border irregularity); C (colour change); D (change in diameter).

Above: Don't forget your beauty sleep.

16 Shadow sense

Q *"I've got dark shadows under my eyes. What's the best way to deal with them?"*

A Dark shadows can be the result of a variety of causes, including fatigue, anaemia, poor digestion and lack of fresh air. They can also be hereditary. If in doubt, consult your doctor for advice. Take steps to ensure you're cutting out the causes – for instance, getting a good night's sleep, and keeping to a low-fat, high-fibre diet.

For special occasions, you can bathe the area with pads soaked in ice-cold water for 15 minutes. This will help lessen the shadow effect temporarily. Or cover shadows by dotting on some concealer.

17 Brown baby

Q *"Is there anything I can do to hang onto my tan for longer?"*

A Just when you want to show off a golden tan, it begins to peel away. This is because your skin is especially dry after sunbathing, and so it sheds its old cells more quickly. You can prolong the colour for a little while longer by applying lots of body lotion in the morning and evening. Apply it while your skin is still damp to make it extra effective. Apply a little fake tan every few days to keep your colour topped up. Or better still, protect your skin by not tanning at all.

18 Sticky situation

Q *"I exercise a lot, and find body odour a problem. How can I prevent it?"*

A Sweating is your body's natural cooling device. Sweat itself has no odour, but it begins to smell when it comes into contact with bacteria on the skin's surface. Keeping underarms hair-free can help prevent sweat from being trapped.

Opt for an antiperspirant deodorant rather than just an ordinary deodorant alone. The antiperspirants help prevent sweating, while the deodorant helps prevent odour. As a result, a product with the combination of the two is highly effective. Also, try to wear natural fibres next to your skin because they help you to stay fresh for longer.

19 Massage magic

Q *"I had a facial massage in a beauty salon. Is there a way I can give myself one at home?"*

A Yes, just like every other part of your body, your face will look better after a bit of exercise, and a massage is the ideal way to give your complexion a workout. Pour a few drops of vegetable oil into the palms of your hands and smooth it onto your face and neck. Make sure your skin is damp, as this makes the oil go on more easily. Then follow these steps:

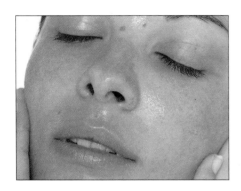

Above: Stroke away the stresses and strains of the day.

- Use the pads of your fingers to stroke upwards from the base of your neck to your chin.
- Continue with long strokes up one side of your face, then the other.
- Now go around your nose and up towards your forehead.
- When you get to your forehead, stroke it across from left to right using one hand. Finish off by gently drawing a circle around each eye using one finger.

20 Stretch marks

Q *"Is there anything I can do to get rid of the stretch marks that have appeared on my tummy, breasts and thighs?"*

A Stretch marks are a sign of your skin's inability to cope with the rapid expansion of flesh underneath. The collagen and elastin fibres underneath actually tear with the sheer strain of it all. They usually make an appearance in times of rapid weight gain, such as puberty and pregnancy. They look quite red when they first appear, although you can take heart that, with time, they fade away to an almost unnoticeable silvery shade.

There's nothing you can do once you've got them, except wait until they start to fade. However, keeping your skin well moisturized can help guard against them. Apply body lotion after a bath or shower, and give it plenty of time to sink in before dressing. Finally, an application of fake tan can be a good disguise for stretch marks that might be on view.

Above: Take time in the bathroom to pamper yourself from top to toe.

BEAUTY BUZZWORDS

If you're confused about the various claims and ingredients in your skin-care products, check out what they mean here in our guide to the most commonly found skin-care jargon.

Allergy-screened

This means that the individual ingredients in the product have gone through exacting tests to ensure that they're safe to use and that there's just the minimum risk of causing allergy.

Aloe vera

The juice from the leaves of this cactus-type plant is often used in skin-care ingredients because of its soothing, protecting and moisturizing qualities.

Anti-oxidants

These work by mopping up and absorbing 'free radicals' from your skin - that is highly reactive molecules that can damage your skin and cause premature ageing. Good anti-oxidants are the ACE vitamins, that is vitamins A, C and E.

Benzoyl peroxide

This is an ingredient commonly used in over-the-counter spot and acne treatments because it gently peels surface skin and unclogs blocked follicles which can cause spots.

Cocoa butter

This comes from the seeds of the cacao tree in tropical climates. Cocoa butter is an excellent moisturizer, especially for dry skin on the body.

Collagen

Collagen is an elastic type of substance in the underlying tissues of your skin that provide support and springiness. Old collagen fibres are less elastic than young collagen, which is one of the main reasons why skin can become less springy as it ages. Collagen is a popular ingredient in skin-care treatments, although it's doubtful if a molecule this size can actually penetrate the skin.

Dermatologically tested

This means the product has been patch tested on a panel of human volunteers to monitor it for any tendency to cause irritation. This means it's usually suitable for sensitive skins.

Exfoliation

Exfoliating means whisking away the top layers of dead surface cells from your skin, making it look brighter and feel smoother. To exfoliate, you massage a gritty exfoliating scrub over damp skin, then rinse away with warm water.

Elastin

These are fibres in the underlying layer of your skin, rather like collagen, which help give it strength and elasticity.

Fruit acids

Also known as AHAs or alpha-hydroxy acids. They're commonly found in natural products, such as fruit, sour milk and wine. AHSs are included in many face creams because they work by breaking down the protein bonds that hold together the dead cells on the skin's surface, to reveal newer, fresher skin underneath.

Below: A pH balanced facial wash will help prevent your skin feeling tight.

Humectants

These ingredients are often found in moisturizers, as they work by attracting moisture to themselves, and so keep the surface layers of your skin well hydrated.

Hypo-allergenic

These products are usually fragrance-free, contain the minimum of colouring agents and no known irritants or sensitizers. This is not a total guarantee that no-one will have an allergic reaction to them. Some people are even allergic to water.

Jojoba oil

Jojoba is a liquid wax obtained from the seeds of a Mexican shrub. It was used for centuries by American Indians. It's a gentle, non-irritant oil which makes an excellent moisturizer as it is easily absorbed into the skin and helps improve the condition of the hair and scalp.

Lanolin free

This means a product doesn't contain the ingredient lanolin – the fat stripped from sheep's wool. At one time it was thought that lanolin was a common skin allergen, although evidence does now seem to show that lanolin is even suitable for sensitive skins.

Liposomes

These are tiny fluid-filled spheres made of the same material that forms cell membranes. Their very small size is said to let them penetrate into the skin's living cells, where they act as delivery parcels that release their active ingredients.

Milia

Another word for whiteheads - small pimples on the skin. Oil produced from the sebaceous glands gathers to form a white plug which is trapped under the skin. You can try to remove these by gently squeezing with tissue-covered fingers or treat them with an antibacterial cream.

Non-comedogenic

A comedo is a blackhead, so this means the product has been screened to eliminate ingredients which can clog the follicles and encourage blackheads and spots. It's particularly useful for oily skins.

Oil of Evening Primrose

The oil taken from the seeds of the evening primrose plant is very useful for helping your skin retain its moisture. It's a wonderful moisturizer, particularly for dry or very dry skins, as it hydrates, protects and soothes. It also improves the skin's overall softness and suppleness. Many sufferers of eczema find it useful.

pH balanced

The pH scale measures the acidity or alkalinity of a solution, with 7 meaning that it is neutral. Any number below that is acidic, and numbers above are alkaline. Healthy skin has a slightly acidic reading, so pH balanced skin-care products are slightly acidic to maintain this natural optimum level.

Retin A

Also known as Retinoic Acid, this is a derivative of vitamin A that has been used for years to treat acne. Now it's available on prescription and to be used under medical supervision, to help reverse the visible signs of ageing on the skin.

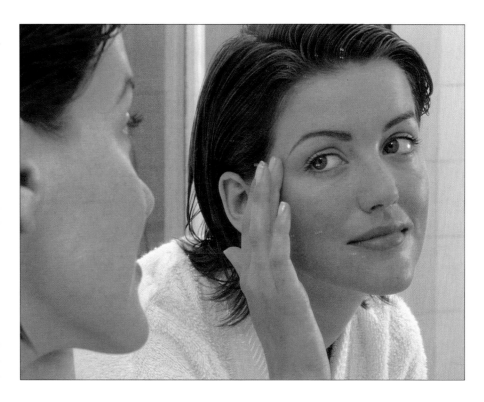

Above: Ensure your mosturizer has an effective sunscreen – check the SPFs to be sure.

S.P.F.

These initials stand for Sun Protection Factor. They'll tell you how long the sun cream or moisturizer will protect you from the sun's burning ultraviolet B rays. The higher the number, the more protection it will give you.

T-panel

This is the area across the forehead and down the centre of the face where the oil glands and sweat glands of the face are most concentrated.

Ultraviolet (UV) rays

Ultraviolet light can damage your skin. UVB rays will burn your skin if you sunbathe too long. UVA rays are strong all year round and cause ageing and wrinkling of the skin. Guard against this with a broad-spectrum sun cream, which contains both UVA and UVB filters.

Vitamin E

This is often used in moisturizers because it can help combat dryness and the signs of ageing. It's also useful for helping to heal scars and burns.

Water soluble

Cleansers are described as water-soluble when they contain oils to dissolve grime and make-up from your skin, with the bonus that they can be easily rinsed away.

Below: Try the healing benefits of vitamin E on your skin.

THE BODY BEAUTIFUL

Caring for your body should mean more than a quick daily shower or bath. Indulge and pamper yourself from top to toe, and acquaint yourself with some of the best and latest body-care techniques. With our special tips and easy programmes, you can achieve a beautiful body simply and easily. Just a little extra care is all it takes to feel better and look better for longer.

HOW WELL DO YOU CARE FOR YOUR BODY?

BODYWISE MEANS BODY BEAUTIFUL

The secret to a beautifully maintained body is to lavish the same care on it as you do on your complexion and make-up. You need to take into account both general maintenance and any special needs it may have. Whatever beauty boosts your body needs, you'll find the help you need in this section of the book.

Throat

Does skin-care stop at your neck?
Is the skin rough and grey?
Do you indulge yourself with special treats to keep your skin in tip-top condition?

Chest

Do you give your breasts the care they need?
Is your chest prone to breakouts?
Do you protect this area of your skin from the harmful rays of the sun?

Arms

Are your elbows grey and dull in tone?
Is the skin soft and supple, or rough and dry?
Do darker hairs on your lower arms need bleaching?

If you remove hair from your underarms, have you found the best method, the one that suits you for convenience and results? Have you found the solution to underarm freshness?

Hands

Do they suffer from too much housework?
Do they need some moisturizing care?
Are your nails neatly filed and shaped?
Would a lick of polish or a French manicure give them a helping hand?

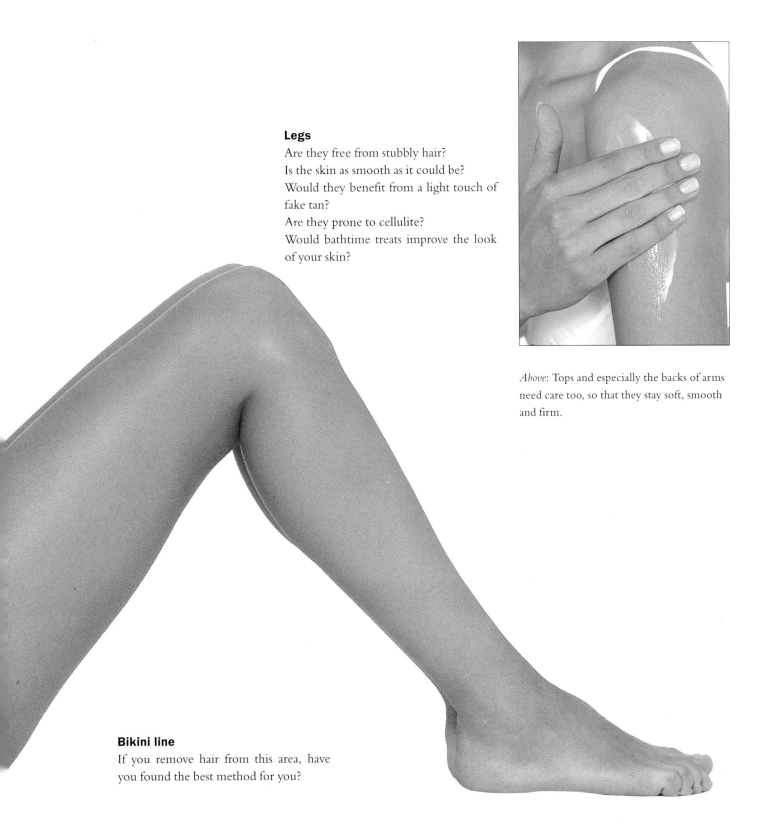

Legs

Are they free from stubbly hair?
Is the skin as smooth as it could be?
Would they benefit from a light touch of fake tan?
Are they prone to cellulite?
Would bathtime treats improve the look of your skin?

Above: Tops and especially the backs of arms need care too, so that they stay soft, smooth and firm.

Bikini line

If you remove hair from this area, have you found the best method for you?

Feet

Are they free from hard skin, corns and calluses?
Are your nails neatly trimmed?
Do you smooth a foot cream on them regularly to ensure that the skin stays soft?

BATHROOM ESSENTIALS

Caring for your body creates endless rewards. So, keep a selection of beauty products on hand to maintain your skin from top to toe on a daily and occasional basis.

BATHING BEAUTY

The time of day and even the time of year will affect what you like using, so why not take the opportunity to try different products, adding the ones you particularly like to those you already know well.

Below: Wonder bars for the body.

Soaps and cleansing bars

These are a cheap and effective way of cleansing your body. If you find them too drying, choose ones that contain moisturizers to minimize these effects. Most people can use ordinary soaps and cleansers without any problem. However, if you have particularly dry or sensitive skin, opt for the pH-balanced variety.

Shower gels and bubble baths

These are mild detergents that help cleanse your body while you soak in the water. There are hundreds of varieties to choose from, including those containing a host of additives, ranging from herbs to essential oils. If you find them too harsh for your skin, look for the ones that offer 2-in-1 benefits – these contain moisturizers as well, to soothe your skin.

Sponges and washcloths

These are useful for lathering up soaps and gels on your skin, and dislodging dirt and grime from your body. Wash your washcloth regularly, and allow it to dry between uses on a wash line or the bathroom window sill. Natural sponges are a more expensive but long-lasting alterna-

tive. Squeeze out afterwards in warm clear water and allow to dry naturally. However, don't underestimate the power of your hands for washing yourself; they keep you in touch with your body and will make you aware of any lumps, bumps and changes in texture that occur.

Bath oils

These are a wonderful beauty boon for those with dry skins. They float on the top of the water, and your entire body becomes covered with a fine film when you step out of the bath. Most cosmetic houses produce a bath oil, but if you're not worried about the fragrance, you can use a few drops of any vegetable oil, such as olive, corn or peanut.

Bath salts

Made from sodium carbonate, these are particularly useful for softening hard water, and for preventing your skin from becoming too dry. Combined with warm water, they're a popular way to soothe away aches and pains.

Below: Bubbles, bubbles – soothe away toils and troubles!

Above: Stock your bathroom shelves for top-to-toe freshness..
Right: Grab yourself some bathroom benefits!

BATHROOM TREATMENTS

As well as a chance to cleanse your body, bath- or shower-time is the perfect opportunity to pamper and polish your skin, and indulge in some beauty treats.

SUPER SOFT SKIN

Try some of these effective body treats on a regular basis!

Body lotions and oils

These can seal moisture into your skin, making it soft and smooth. Especially concentrate them on drier areas such as feet, elbows and knees. Oilier and normal skins benefit from lotions, while oils and creams suit drier skins.

Exfoliating scrubs

These help combat the rough patches and blackheads that can appear on your skin. Use once or twice a week in the bath or shower, rinsing away the excess with clear warm water.

Pumice stone

These are made from very porous volcanic rock, and work best if you lather up with soap before rubbing at hardened areas of skin in a circular motion. Don't rub too fiercely or else you'll make the skin sore. A little and often is best.

Loofah or back-brush

Loofahs are useful as exfoliators, and their length makes them great for scrubbing difficult-to-reach areas like the back. They're actually the pod of an Egyptian plant and need a bit of care if they're to last. Rinse and drain them thoroughly after use to stop them going black and mouldy. Avoid rinsing them in vinegar and lemon juice as this can be too harsh for these once-living things. Back-brushes are easier to care for; you simply rinse them in cool water after use and leave them to dry.

Right: Get back to basics with a brush to reach difficult areas.

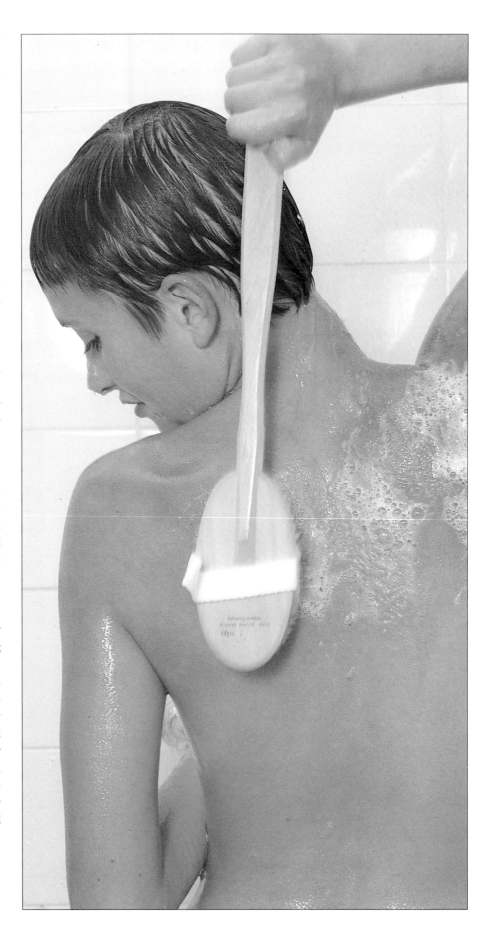

GET FRESH!

From cleaning your teeth to preventing underarm odour, here's the lowdown.

A toothbrush

You need to choose the right toothbrush to get the maximum benefit from it. A nylon brush is best, as bristle splits and loses its shape quickly. Choose one with a small head so you can easily clean your back teeth. A soft or medium brush is best as the harder brushes may damage the tooth enamel and gums. Change your toothbrush regularly, about every month.

Dental floss

Use floss at least once a day to clean between the teeth where the toothbrush can't reach. Waxed floss is best as it's less likely to catch on fillings or uneven edges. To floss, wind a short length around the second finger of each hand. Slide it gently down between two of the teeth, taking care to press it against the side of the tooth. Then gently slide it upwards out of the teeth, removing any food particles with it. Repeat between all of the teeth.

Antiperspirant deodorant

Deodorants don't stop perspiration – they only stop the bacteria from decomposing the sweat. If you perspire heavily, use an antiperspirant or even better an antiperspirant deodorant. The antiperspirant part prevents the production of sweat. Never use on inflamed or broken skin or immediately after shaving.

Talcum powder

Talcum powder is made from finely ground magnesium silicate, usually perfumed. It has been out of fashion in recent years, which is a shame as it makes you smell fresh and helps you slide into your clothes, but it is no substitute for a thorough job with the towel, especially between the toes.

Right: Powder power for fresh, dry skin!

FRESH IDEAS FOR THE SHOWER & BATH

Once you've armed yourself with some bathroom basics, try these water-baby treats to boost your body, beauty and mood.

BATH-TIME TREATS

Soaking in a warm bath has to be one of the most popular ways to relax. You can literally feel your cares disappear as you sink into the soothing water. However you can also use bathtime for a variety of other benefits and beauty boosters.

The sleepy "sitz" bath

The combination of hot and cold temperatures is an effective way of helping you get to sleep. Try a "sitz" bath, which helps you relax by drawing energy away from your head and stopping your mind from racing. Here's how to create your own "sitz" bath:

● Ensure the bathroom is warm, then fill the bath with 7.5-10 cm (3-4 in) of cold water.

● Wrap the top half of your body in a warm sweater or towel, then immerse your hips and bottom in the cold water for 30 seconds.

● Get out of the bath, pat yourself dry, then climb into bed and fall asleep.

Learning to relax

Turn bathtime into an aromatherapy treat by adding relaxing essential oils such as camomile and lavender to the water. Just add a few drops once you've run the bath, then lie back, inhale the vapours and relax. Salts and bubble baths that contain sea minerals and kelp also have a relaxing effect, and purify your skin, too. Bathe by candlelight and listen to soothing music to make it even more of a treat. Put on eye pads and relax for 10 minutes.

Be a natural beauty

You don't have to splash out on expensive bath additives – try making your own:

● Soothe irritated skin by adding a cup of cider vinegar to the running water.

● A cup of powdered milk will soothe rough skin.

Above: Bathtime is more fun if you share it!

● Add a cupful of oatmeal or bran to cleanse, whiten and soothe your skin.

Sleek skin

Smooth your body with body oil before getting into the bath. After soaking for 10 minutes, rub your skin with a soft wash-cloth – you'll be amazed at how much dead skin you remove!

Fabulous fragrance

Add free samples of perfume to a bath. It won't cost you anything and will smell wonderfully luxurious.

SHOWER-TIME TREATS

Showers are a wonderful opportunity to cleanse your body quickly, cheaply and to wake yourself up. Here are some of the other benefits.

Circulation booster

Switch on the cold water before finishing your shower to help boost your circulation. Strangely, it will also make you feel warmer once you get out of the shower! It also works well if you concentrate the blasts of cold water on cellulite-prone areas, as this stimulates the sluggish circulation in these spots.

Boosting benefits

If you pat yourself dry after a bath, it'll help you to unwind, whereas briskly rubbing your skin with a towel will help to invigorate you.

Shower sensation

Add a few drops of essential oils to the floor of the shower itself. As they evaporate you will find that you're surrounded by a sensuous-smelling mist while you wash your body.

Above: Splish! Splash! Relax and have fun in the bath.
Right: Turn a daily shower into a real power shower.

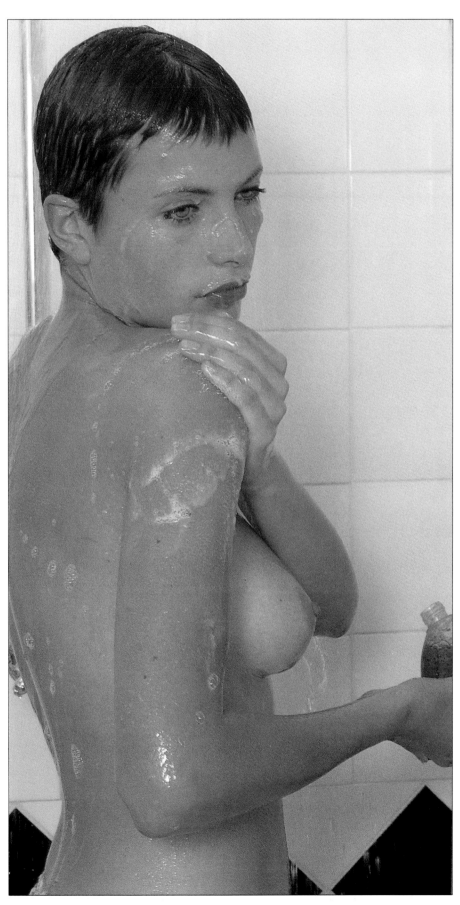

SCRUB YOUR WAY TO SMOOTHER SKIN

Improve your skin-tone from top to toe with the regular use of a body scrub. This quick treatment is easy to do and boasts great results.

The chances are, even if your skin isn't prone to spottiness or flaky patches, it will suffer from dullness and poor condition from time to time. This is where body scrubs and exfoliaters come into their own. They work by shifting dead cells from the surface of your skin, revealing the younger, fresher ones underneath. This process also stimulates the circulation of blood in the skin tissues, giving it a rosy glow.

METHODS TO TRY

There are lots of different ways you can exfoliate your body – so there's one to suit every budget and preference.

● Your first option is to buy an exfoliating scrub, which is a cream or gel based product containing tiny abrasive particles. Look for the type with rounded particles which won't scratch and irritate delicate skin. Simply massage the scrub into damp skin, then rinse away thoroughly with lots of warm water.

● A bath mitt, loofah or sisal mitt are a cinch to use, and cost-effective too. They can be quite harsh on the skin if you press too hard, so go easily at first. Rinse them well after use, and allow them to dry naturally. Simply sweep over your body when you're in the shower or bath.

● Your ordinary washcloth or bath sponge can also double up as an exfoliater. Lather up with plenty of soap or shower gel, and massage over damp skin before rinsing away with clear water.

● Copy what health spas do, and keep a large tub of natural sea salt by the shower. Scoop up a handful when you get in, and massage over your skin. Rinse away thoroughly afterwards.

● You can also make your own body scrub at home by mixing sea salt with body oil or olive oil. Allow the mixture to soak into your skin for a few minutes to allow the edges of the salt to dissolve before massaging in, then rinsing away.

● Body brushes are also useful. The best way to use them is on dry skin before you get in the bath or shower, as this is particularly good for loosening dead skin cells. You can also use them in the water, lathering them up with soap or gel.

Again, just take care that you don't get too enthusiastic with the brushing and scrub your skin so vigorously that it becomes sore.

Perfect your technique

Whichever method you use, the best thing to do is concentrate on problem areas such as upper arms, thighs, bottom, heels and elbows. Also sweep over the rest of your body. However, go gently on delicate areas of skin, such as the inner arms, stomach and inner thighs. Work in large strokes, in the direction of your heart.

Above: Keep a sisal mitt to hand for super soft skin.
Right: Regular exfoliating works!

Oilier skin types will benefit from exfoliation 2-3 times a week, while once a week is sufficient for other types. Never exfoliate broken, inflamed or acne-prone skins.

After exfoliating, always apply body lotion to seal moisture into the new fresh skin you've exposed.

BEAUTY TIP
For super-soft skin fast, you should massage your body with oil first before getting into the bath or shower. Then follow the exfoliating method you prefer.

SIMPLE STEPS TO SOFTER SKIN

Slick on a body moisturizer to create a wonderfully silky body. Add a moisturizing body treat every day to your beauty regime, and you'll soon reap the benefits.

MOISTURIZING MATTERS

Just as you choose a moisturizer for your face with care, you should opt for the best formulation suited to the skin type on your body.

● Gels are the lightest formulation and are perfect for very hot days or oilier skin types. They contain a lot of nourishing ingredients even though they're very easy to wear.

● Lotions and oils are good for most skin-types, and easy to apply, as they're not sticky.

● Creams give better results for those with dry skins, especially very dry areas.

Make the most of body moisturizer

● Apply using firm strokes to boost your circulation as you massage in the product.

● Apply the moisturizer straight onto clean, damp skin – after a bath or shower is the ideal time. This helps seal extra moisture into the upper layers of your skin, making is softer than ever.

● Soften cracked feet by rubbing them with rich body lotion, pulling on a pair of cotton socks and heading for bed. They'll be beautifully soft by the next morning!

● Concentrate on rubbing moisturizer into particularly dry areas, like heels, knees and elbows. The calves of the legs are also very prone to dryness because there aren't that many oil glands there.

● If you don't have time to apply moisturizer after your bath, simply add a few drops of body oil to the water. When you step out of the bath, your skin will be coated with a fine film of nourishing oil. Remember to rinse the bath well afterwards to prevent you from slipping the next time you take a dip!

● Your breasts don't have any supportive muscle from the nipple to the collarbone and skin is very fine here. Firming creams won't work miracles, but can help maintain the elasticity and suppleness in this delicate area. Regular applications of body lotion can also have similar effects.

Smelling scentsational!

Opt for a scented body lotion as a wonderful treat. They can be longer-lasting than the actual fragrances themselves. Alternatively, use them as part of "fragrance layering". This simply means taking advantage of the various scent formulations available. Start with a scented bath oil and soap, move onto the matching body lotion and powder, and leave the house wearing the fragrance itself sprayed onto pulse points.

However, be careful you don't clash fragrances. Opt for unscented products if you're also wearing perfume, unless you're going to be wearing a matching scented body lotion. You don't want cheaper products to compete with your more expensive perfume.

Above left: Opt for the light touch with a moisturizing gel.
Right: Take the time before dressing to moisturize your skin. Why not apply body lotion and then leave your skin to absorb it whilst you clean your teeth or dry your hair?

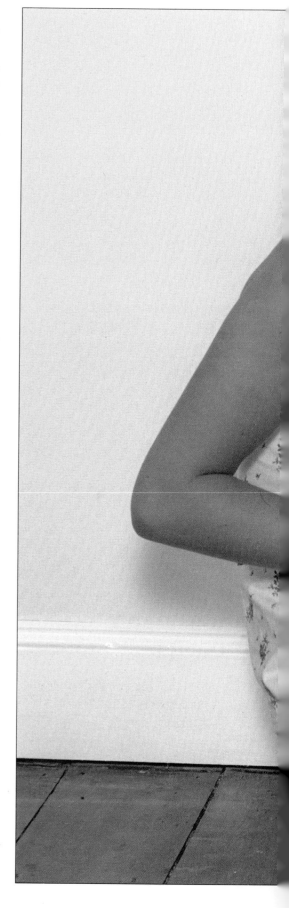

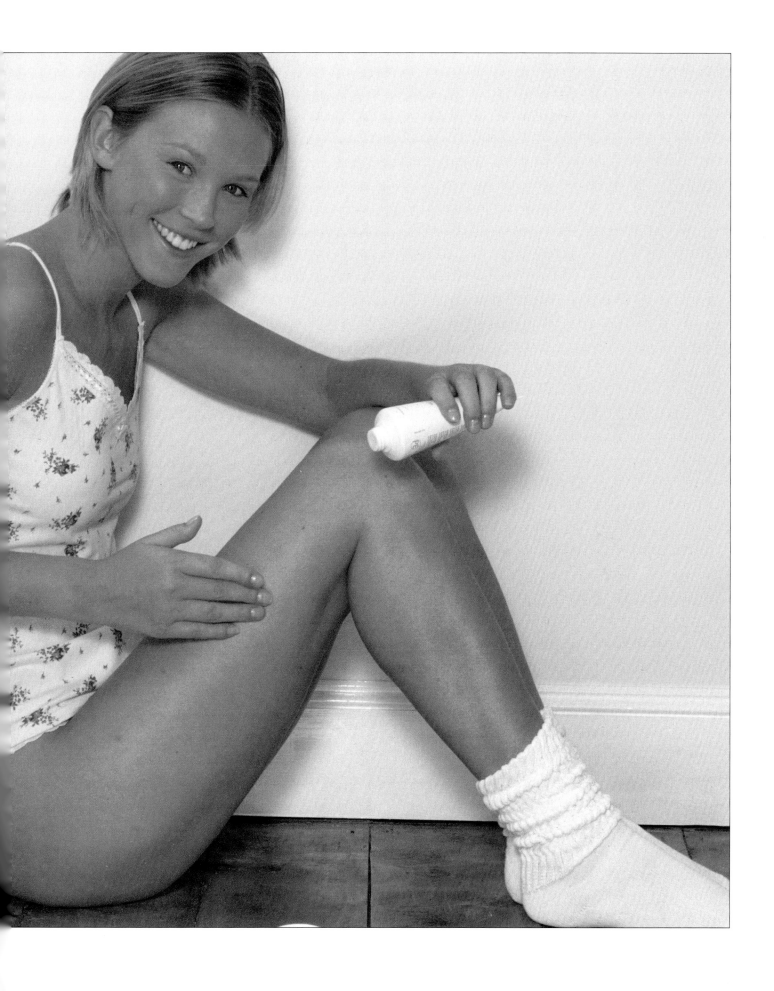

BE A SMOOTHIE!

Hair on a woman's body is quite natural, but fashion and cultural practices mean that it's usually removed. Here are the main removal methods.

THE KEY METHODS

There are several different ways to tackle superfluous hair.

Shaving

Shaving works by cutting the hair at the skin surface with a razor blade. It's best for legs and underarms.

Pros: Cheap, quick and painless.

Cons: Regrowth appears again quickly, within a couple of days.

> ### SHAVING TIPS
> • Combine with a moisturizing shave foam or gel for a close shave. Moisturize afterwards to soothe your skin.
>
> • A closer shave means a less frequent one. Let the shaving cream get to work and soften the hair for a few moments before using your razor.

Tweezing

Tweezing plucks out hairs, one at a time. Because it's time-consuming, it's best for small areas like eyebrows, or for removing the odd stray hair missed by waxing.

Pros: Good control for shaping.

Cons: Can be painful and may make skin slightly reddened for a while afterwards. You also need to remember to check the area regularly in a mirror to see that you don't need to re-tweezer.

> ### TWEEZER TIP
> Hold a warm washcloth over the area of hair to dampen and soften it first, and open the pores – this will make tweezing easier. Or, press an ice cube over the area to anaesthetize it first if you find it really painful!

Waxing

This method uproots the hair from below the skin's surface. Either wax is smoothed onto the skin and removed with strips, or pre-prepared wax strips are used. This is a form of hair removal that can be safely used on any part of your body.

Pros: The results last for 2-6 weeks.

Cons: Can be painful and there's the risk of soreness and of ingrowing hairs. Also, hair has to be left to grow until it's long enough to wax, so you have a time when the hairs have grown back. If the hair is too short, it won't come out, or will be removed patchily.

> ### WAXING TIPS
> • After waxing the bikini area, apply an antibacterial cream to prevent infection or a rash.
>
> • Wear loose clothing after waxing.
>
> • Never wax on a sore area.

Depilatory creams

These contain chemicals that weaken the hair at the skin's surface, so hair can be wiped away. Simply apply, leave for about 5-10 minutes, then rinse away. (Check the packaging for exact instructions.) You can use a depilatory cream anywhere, especially as some companies produce different formulations for specific areas.

Do a patch test 24 hours before using the product to make sure it won't cause irritation or an allergy.

Pros: It's cheap, and the results last a bit longer than a razor – up to a week.

Cons: Can be messy, and takes time. The smell of some products can be off-putting although formulations have improved.

Bleaching

Although this isn't technically hair removal, it's a great way to make superfluous hair less noticeable. A solution of hydrogen peroxide solution is used to lighten the hair, which makes it less visible. Bleaching is best for use on your arms, upper lip and face.

Above: Sugaring – the sweeter solution to superfluous hair.
Right: Shaving is the no-fuss option for silky smooth legs.

Pros: Results last between 2-6 weeks, and there's no regrowth.

Cons: Not suitable for coarse hair.

> ### BLEACHING TIP
> If using a new product, do a patch test on your skin first to ensure you don't react to the product's bleaching agents.

Sugaring

Works in a similar way to waxing, but uses a paste made from sugar, lemon and water. It's well known in the Middle East, and is growing in popularity elsewhere.

Pros: Has the same benefits as waxing and can be used anywhere on the body.

Cons: Can be fairly painful and there is a risk of ingrowing hairs.

Electrolysis

A needlelike probe conducts an electric current into the hair follicle, inactivating it. This method is best for small areas such as breasts and face. Go to a qualified practitioner (and ask to see their certificates).

Pros: A permanent solution.

Cons: Expensive and is more painful for some people than others, depending upon your pain threshold. You may find that you are more sensitive to the pain just before or during your period.

INDULGE YOURSELF WITH AROMATHERAPY

Many more of us are waking up to the benefits of aromatherapy these days, and for good reason. It's wonderful to use, the products are easily available, and they can give immediate results. It's no surprise then, that it's one of the most popular therapies around.

Aromatherapy uses essential oils, that are the distilled essences of herbs, plants, flowers and trees. These oils smell wonderful, and are a pleasure to use. It's this smell that usually attracts people to them for treating a variety of physical and mental conditions, from skin infections to stress. There are three main ways to use essential oils.

In your bath

Add 5-10 drops of your chosen oil to your bath, then sink in and relax. Inhaling the wonderful aromas will soothe your mind, and the oils will also have a beneficial effect on your skin and body. Only pour oil into the bath once it's been run, or the oil will evaporate with the heat of the water and you'll lose the therapeutic properties before you even get in!

For massage

Mix 3-4 drops of essential oil into 10 ml (2 teaspoons) of a neutral carrier oil such as sweet almond oil, and use to massage your body – or ask someone else to massage you! Alternatively, choose one of the many pre-blended oils currently on the market. Most aromatherapists believe that you're naturally drawn to the oils that will do you most good at that time – so why not start by experimenting with some of the oils described here.

To perfume your room

Fragrance your room and indulge in the beneficial scent. Clay burners are readily available to diffuse oils into the air. You add the oil to some water in the bowl at the top, then light the night candle underneath. This will prevent the oil from burning and help to create sweet-smelling steam. Alternatively, place 6 drops of your favourite oil in a small bowl of water and put it in a warm place. There are also ring diffusers you can put on light bulbs, or you can add a few drops of oil to the water in a plant sprayer, and use it to spritz the room whenever you like.

WONDERFUL OILS TO TRY

There are several hundred essential oils to choose from, so it can be confusing knowing which ones to try. These are some useful ones to start with:

Essential oil	Benefits	Use for
Chamomile	calming	headaches and anxiety
Mandarin	calming, refreshing	digestive problems
Eucalyptus	decongestant	colds
Lavender	calming and balancing	stress, colds, headaches, P.M.S.
Peppermint	refreshing	indigestion and sickness
Rose	soothing	depression
Rosemary	antiseptic and stimulating	aches and pains
Sandalwood	relaxing	stress, dry skin-care
Tea tree	anti-bacterial	pimples and cold sores
Ylang ylang	love potion	boosting sex drive

Below: Flower power – treat yourself with fragrant oils from flowers, plants and herbs.

AROMATHERAPY TIPS

1 If you don't want to buy individual essential oils buy them ready-blended, or treat yourself to bath and body products that contain them.

2 Some oils are thought to carry some risk during pregnancy. For this reason, consult a qualified aromatherapist for advice if you are expecting a child and want to use essential oils.

3 Don't try to treat medical conditions with them – always consult your GP.

4 Essential oils can be expensive, but remember that a little goes a long way.

5 Don't apply essential oils to the skin undiluted as they're far too concentrated in this form, and can result in inflammation. The only exception is lavender, which can be used directly on the skin for insect bites and stings. Otherwise essential oils should be mixed with a carrier oil.

6 Don't take essential oils internally. Essential oils are approximately 50 to 100 times more powerful than the plant they were extracted from.

7 Don't apply oils to areas of broken, inflamed or recently scarred skin.

8 Whichever method of aromatherapy you use, shut the door to the room to prevent the aroma from escaping!

9 For immediate results from aromatherapy, try inhaling the steam. Add about 4 drops of your chosen oil to a bowl of hot water, lean over it and cover your head with a towel. Inhale deeply for about 5 minutes.

10 Place a few drops of your favourite oil on a tissue, so you can inhale it whenever you like. Eucalyptus is great if your sinuses are blocked and you have a cold. Alternatively, sprinkle a few drops of chamomile or lavender on your pillow to help you sleep.

Top left: Special essential oils – for a sensual experience.

Top right: Dilute them in light carrier oil to pamper the body.

Right: Try a soothing aromatherapy bath, and let your cares float away.

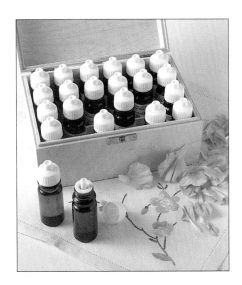

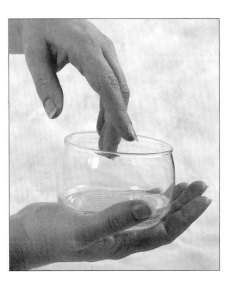

BEAT THE CELLULITE PROBLEM

It's not just plumper, older women who suffer from "orange-peel skin" on their thighs, hips, bottom and even tummy – many slim, young women suffer, too. Despite what you may have heard, there is no miracle cure for cellulite, but there are some effective and practical things you can do to see great results.

FACTS ON CELLULITE

Experts differ about what exactly causes cellulite. It seems likely that it's an accumulation of fat, fluid and toxins trapped into the hardened network of elastin and collagen fibres in the deeper levels of your skin. This causes the dimpled effect and feel of cellulite areas. These areas also tend to feel cold to the touch because the flow of blood is constricted and the lymph system, which is responsible for eliminating toxins, can't work properly. This can worsen the problem and make the cellulite feel puffy and spongy.

HAVE I GOT CELLULITE?

Try squeezing the skin of your upper thigh between your thumb and index finger. If the flesh feels lumpy and looks bumpy, you have cellulite. Further clues may be that these areas look whiter, and feel colder than elsewhere on your legs.

Common causes

Cellulite can be caused and/or aggravated by the following:
- A poor diet is full of toxins and puts the body under great strain to get rid of vast quantities of waste. Also, an unhealthy low-fibre, high-fat diet means that the body's digestive system can't work effectively to expel toxins from the body.
- Stress and lack of exercise make your body sluggish and can slow down blood circulation and the lymphatic system.
- Hereditary factors – if your mother has cellulite, it's a fair bet you will have, too.
- Hormones, such as the contraceptive pill or hormone replacement therapy, may be contributory.

TAKING THE SENSIBLE APPROACH

There are dozens of products around designed to deal with cellulite but to really tackle the problem you should follow a three-pronged approach, combining:
- Circulation boosting tactics
- Diet
- Exercise.

Boost your circulation

Here are several ways to boost your circulation and your lymphatic system. Whichever one you choose, aim to follow it for at least 5 minutes a day.
- Use a soft body brush on damp or dry skin, brushing in long sweeping movements over the afflicted area, and working in the direction of the heart.
- Use a massage glove or rough sisal mitt in the same way as above.
- Use a cellulite cream. These usually contain natural ingredients such as horse chestnut, ivy and caffeine to pep up your circulation. However, you can make them doubly effective by massaging them in thoroughly with your fingertips. Or, some cellulite creams come with their own plastic or rubber hand-held mitts to help boost the circulation.

> **MAKE YOUR OWN CELLULITE CREAM**
> Some women swear by aromatherapy to treat their cellulite. There are many ready blended oils on the market, but you can make your own. Just add two drops each of rosemary and fennel essential oils to three teaspoons of carrier oil, such as almond oil. Massage this mixture daily thoroughly into the affected areas.

Follow a detox diet

To detoxify your body you need to follow a healthy low-fat, high fibre diet – one that contains plenty of fresh fruit and vegetables. The great news is, if you have any excess weight to lose it will naturally fall away by following these rules.
- Eat at least 5 servings of fresh fruit and vegetables every day.
- Cut down on the amount of fat you eat. For instance, grill rather than fry foods, and cut off visible fat from meat. For many foods you buy, look out for a low-fat alternative.
- Water cleanses your system and flushes toxins from body cells, so drink at least 2 litres (quarts) of pure water every day.
- Change from caffeine-laden tea and coffee to herbal teas and decaffeinated coffee. Sip pure fruit juices rather than fizzy drinks.
- Steer clear of alcohol as much as possible as it adversely affects your liver – your body's main de-toxifier.
- Drink a glass of hot water containing the juice of a fresh lemon when you get up in the morning – it's a wonderful way to detoxify your body.
- Avoid sugary snacks between meals – eat a piece of fruit, raw vegetables or rice cakes instead.

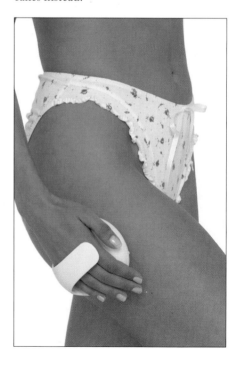

Right: Pep up your circulation and lymphatic system to help beat that cellulite.

Step up your exercise

Exercise will boost your sluggish circulation and lymphatic system, and encourage your body to get rid of the toxins causing your cellulite. Do a regular aerobic workout, exercising for 20-40 minutes, 3-5 times a week, and choose from these: brisk walking, jogging, swimming, cycling, tennis, badminton, aerobic classes or running. (It is always wise to consult your doctor before embarking on a new form of exercise.)

Tone it up!

On a more specific level, you can also try these exercises to firm up your legs and give them a better shape. Carried out daily, they will help you win the cellulite battle.

Bottom toner

Lie on your front with your hands on top of one another, resting your chin on them if you wish. Raise one leg about 13 cm (5 in) off the floor, and hold for a count of 10. Bring your leg back to the floor, and repeat 15-20 times with each leg.

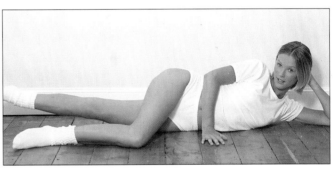

Inner thigh toner

Lie on your side on the floor, supporting your head with your arm. With your top leg resting on the floor in front, raise the lower leg off the floor as far as you can without straining, then gently lower it again. Repeat 10 times, then turn over and work the other leg.

Hip toner

Stand sideways with your hand resting on a chair. Your knees should be slightly bent and your shoulders relaxed. Slowly raise your right leg, keeping your body and raised foot facing forward. Carefully and slowly lower your leg, and then repeat this movement 10 times. Turn round and repeat with the other leg.

Outer thigh toner

Lie on your side, supporting your head with your hand. Bend your lower leg behind you and tilt your hips slightly forward. Place your other hand on the floor in front of you for balance. Slowly lift your upper leg, then bring it down to touch the lower one, and repeat this action 6 times. Repeat on the other side.

BROWNIE POINTS IN THE SUN

There's nothing that lifts your spirits like spending time in the sunshine. However, you need to take special care of your skin against the potential dangers of suntanning. The secret is to give your skin the protection it needs, whilst you gradually develop a light attractive colour.

THE RIGHT PRODUCT

There are so many sun creams and lotions on the market, but it's essential to use the right one because going for the burn can age your skin and increase your chances of skin cancer. So, play safe by following our two-step plan.

STEP 1: KNOW YOUR SPFS

The initials SPF stand for Sun Protection Factor. The higher the number of the SPF, the more protection the product will give you from the burning ultraviolet B (UVB) rays. For instance, an SPF 2 will let you stay out in the sun for twice as long as you usually would without burning, whereas an SPF 8 will let you stay out eight times as long.

STEP 2: GO BY SKIN-TYPE

To decide which SPF suits you, you need to know how vulnerable your skin is to the sun's UVB rays. Dermatologists divide skins into six types, each needing a different level of protection. By knowing your skin-type you can ensure it is always well protected, wherever you travel.

Skin-type 1

Always burns, never tans. Fair-skinned, usually with freckles. Red or blonde hair. Typical Irish or Anglo-Saxon skin-type.
UK/North Europe: Total sunblock, or keep out of the sun.
USA/Tropics/Africa: Total sunblock.
Mediterranean : Total sunblock.

Skin-type 2

Burns easily and tans with difficulty. Fair hair and pale skin. Typical North European skin-type.
UK/North Europe: Start with SPF 20 and use sunblock on delicate areas. Progress gradually to SPF 15.
USA/Tropics/Africa: Start with sunblock and progress gradually to SPF 20.
Mediterranean: Start with SPF 20, use sunblock on delicate areas, and progress gradually to SPF 15.

Skin-type 3

Sometimes burns but tans well. Light brown hair and medium skin tone. Again, a typical North European skin-type.
UK/North Europe: Start with SPF 10 and progress to SPF 8.
USA/Tropics/Africa: Start with SPF 20, moving to SPF 15, then SPF 10.
Mediterranean: Start with SPF 15, moving to SPF 10.

Skin-type 4

Occasionally burns but tans easily. Usually with brown hair and eyes, and olive skin. The typical Mediterranean skin-type.
UK/North Europe: Start with SPF 8, moving to SPF 6.
USA/Tropics/Africa: Start with SPF 15, moving to SPF 8.
Mediterranean: Start with SPF 10, moving to SPF 6.

Skin-type 5

Hardly ever burns and tans very easily. Dark eyes, dark hair and olive skin. A typical Middle Eastern or Asian skin-type.
UK/North Europe: Use SPF 6 throughout.
USA/Tropics/Africa: Start with SPF 8 and move to SPF 6.
Mediterranean: Start with SPF 8 and move to SPF 6.

Skin-type 6

Almost never burns. Has dark hair, eyes and skin. Typical African or Afro-Caribbean skin-type.
UK/North Europe: No sunscreen needed.
USA/Tropics/Africa: Start with SPF 8, moving to SPF 6.
Mediterranean: Use SPF 6 throughout.

A TIP FOR STAR QUALITY!

Many companies producing suntan products have recently introduced a star rating system. This indicates how well the product will protect you against the UVA rays of the sun – the ones that are responsible for the signs of ageing, such as lines and wrinkles. It is worth catching onto if you seriously want to keep your skin young-looking. The more stars your suntan product has, the better.

★

1 star gives moderate UVA protection.

★★

2 stars give good UVA protection.

★★★

3 stars give superior UVA protection.

★★★★

4 stars give maximum UVA protection.

If a product doesn't have this star rating, then doublecheck on the packaging that it does offer good UVA protection.

YOUR SAFE TAN PLAN

● Apply suntan lotion (block) before you go into the sun, and before you dress, to ensure that you don't miss any areas.
● Gradually build up the time you spend in the sun. Never be tempted to burn – it's a sign of skin damage.
● Stay out of the sun between 12 noon and 3 o'clock when the sun is at its hottest. Move into the shade or cover up with a t-shirt and broad-brimmed hat.
● If you're playing a lot of sport or swimming, choose a special sports formula or waterproof formulation.
● Lips need a good lip screen to protect them from burning and chapping.
● Like skin-care ranges, there are hypoallergenic products around, so ask at your pharmacist.

Opposite page, right: Protect and survive. Guard against ageing and the burning rays of the sun with an effective sun cream.
Opposite page far right: Go for the glow with a light golden tan.
Photographs courtesy of Nivea.

JOIN THE BROWNIES –
WITH A FAKE TAN!

The safest tan of all is one that comes out of a bottle! There are three main ways to fake a tan.

Bronzing powders

For use on your face, these act in the same way as a blusher. Make sure that the one you use is not too pearlized, or you'll really shimmer in the sunshine.

Wash-off tanners

These are the simplest way to create an instant tan on your face and body. You simply smooth on the cream, then wash it away at the end of the day.

Self-tanners

If you haven't tried these formulations for years because you remember the awful smell, orange colour and streaky results, then you'll be pleasantly surprised at the dramatic improvements that have been made. In fact, choose carefully, and you'll create an acceptable alternative to the real thing. These products contain an active ingredient called dihydroxyacetone (DHA), which is absorbed by surface skin cells, and turns brown in the presence of oxygen – which creates the "tan". This process usually takes 3-4 hours, and the effects last until these skin cells are naturally shed – which can be from a few days right up to a week.

SELF-TANNING TIPS

● Use a body scrub first to rub away the dead flaky skin that can soak up colour and create a patchy finish.

● Massage in plenty of body lotion over the area to be treated. This will combat any remaining dry areas, and give a smooth surface on which to apply the tanning lotion.

● If there's a shade choice, go with the lighter one, because you can always apply more to get a darker colour.

● Use only a small amount of the product at a time – you can always apply a second layer later on.

● Work the product firmly into the skin until it feels completely dry. Any excess left on the surface is likely to go patchy.

● If you've applied self-tan to your body, wipe areas that don't normally tan with damp cottonwool (cotton) – armpits, nipples, soles of feet and fingers. On the face, work the cottonwool (cotton) around eyebrows, hairline and jawline.

● While there are self-tanning products which offer some protection from the sun until your wash your skin, it's best to use them in conjunction with the best sunscreen for your skin-type.

THE MAGIC OF
MAKE-UP

While models and movie stars may have a gaggle of make-up artists to hand, real women don't. The key to making up successfully is to understand how to enhance your features, using the best cosmetic formulations and colours around. This doesn't mean spending a small fortune on the latest season's colours and promotions. Instead, it means analysing what will work for you, your colouring and your lifestyle, then making your purchases. If you wise up on the best of products around, brushing up your application techniques and give yourself time to experiment, you can find the perfect look for you. And, once you've mastered the basics, you can solve your own particular beauty problems, and try out some inspirational make-up ideas – just for fun!

MAKE-UP FOR EVERY WOMAN

Being considered beautiful today no longer means conforming to one accepted ideal. The contemporary approach to beauty places the emphasis firmly on the individual, and her own particular needs, aspirations and lifestyle. For although every woman is concerned to some extent about how she looks, everyone is very different. For instance, the make-up needs of a blue-eyed blonde are not the same as a dark-eyed woman with an Oriental skin-tone.

The great news is that make-up can be used to enhance everyone's features. Applied with a light touch it should create a subtle emphasis, rather than a mask disguising the features.

PRODUCT KNOW-HOW

No two women are alike. When we're buying a pair of jeans, we don't just pick the same size, colour and pair as our sister, because we have different requirements. Make-up is the same. We need to choose carefully from the vast array of products and formulations around to create a look that's made-to-measure for our own complexions and features. Simply buying the most expensive product on the shelves is no guarantee of success, as it may not be the most suitable for your colouring or skin-type.

These pages will take you through the myriad of bottles, compacts and colours around, and guide you on how to find the ones that work the best for you, and how to apply them.

Tailor-made make-up

The perfect make-up for you will be effortless once you choose the correct shades for your skin-tone and hair colour. It'll also work wonderfully, because you'll still look like you, only better! Checking your hair colour is easy – whether or not it's natural or comes out of a bottle. Deciding whether your skin is "warm" or "cool" can be slightly more difficult – however, there is an easy way to check. Simply look in a mirror and hold a piece of gold and a piece of silver in front of

your face. These can just as easily be pieces of foil or costume jewellery as the real thing. The right metal will bring a healthy glow to your skin, whereas the wrong one will make it look grey. If gold suits your skin, then it's "warm" toned. If silver suits it, it's "cool" toned. A further clue is how well you tan in the sun – cool skin-tones tend to colour less easily.

Inspirational ideas

Sometimes make-up should be used just for the sheer fun of it. Try out a different look for a special occasion, bringing out the make-up artist in you. Whether you want to create an impact in the office, or turn heads at a party, there are lots of ideas to help you put on the perfect face.

Above: Every woman can use make-up to emphasize her best features.
Right: We're all different. What works for one woman may not work for another. Understanding this helps you to bring out the best in yourself.

Problem solvers

Don't just read about them but actually put new ideas into practice! Brush up on tips and tricks to help you maximize your looks, and deal with your own particular beauty needs. Perhaps you need a new look on a budget, speedy ideas or some expert help. Spend a little time to make the most of yourself.

FOUNDATION THAT FITS

Many women avoid foundation, because they're scared of an unnatural, mask-like effect. In fact, finding the right product for you is simpler than you might think. There are two keys to success, the first is to pick the right formulation, and the second is to choose the perfect shade for your skin.

FIND YOUR FORMULATION

Long gone are the days when you could only buy heavy pancake foundation. Now you can choose from many formulations, so you can get the best coverage for your particular skin-type. Here's what's on offer, and who they're best for.

Tinted moisturizers

These are a cross between a moisturizer and a foundation, as they'll soothe your skin while giving a little coverage. They're ideal for young or clear skins. They're also great in the summer, when you want a sheer effect or to even out a fading tan. Unlike other foundations, you can blend tinted moisturizers on with your fingertips.

Liquid foundations

These are the most popular and versatile of all foundation types, because they smooth on easily and offer a natural-looking coverage. They suit all but the driest skins. If you have oily skin or suffer from breakouts, look for an oil-free liquid foundation, to cover affected areas without aggravating them.

Cream foundations

These are thick, rich and moisturizing, making them ideal for dry or mature skins. As they have a fairly heavy texture, make sure you blend them well into your skin with a damp cosmetic sponge.

Mousse foundations

Again these are quite moisturizing, and ideal for drier skins. The best way is to dab a little of the product onto the back of your hand, then dot onto your skin with a sponge.

Above: Spend time finding the right foundation colour for you.

Compact foundations

These are all-in-one formulations, which already contain powder. They come in a compact, usually with their own sponge for application. However, they actually give a lighter finish than you'd expect. They're great on all but dry skin-types.

Stick foundations

These are the original foundation, dating back to the days of Hollywood. They have a heavy texture, and so are best confined for use on badly blemished or scarred skin. Dot a little foundation directly onto the affected area, then blend gently with a damp sponge.

SHADE SELECTION

Once you've chosen the ideal formulation for you, you're ready to choose the perfect matching shade to your skin. At last cosmetic companies have woken up to the fact that not everyone has an "American tan" complexion! Now, there is a good selection of foundation shades from a pink-toned English rose to a yellow-hued, olive skin, as well as from the palest skin to the darkest one. Here's how

to select the perfect one for you.

● Ensure you're in natural daylight when trying out foundation colours, so you can see exactly how your skin will look once you leave the shop or counter.
● Select a couple of shades to try, which look as though they'll match your skin.
● Don't try foundation on your hand or on your wrist – they're a different colour to your face.
● Stroke a little colour onto your jawline to ensure you get a tone that will blend with your neck as well as your face. The shade that seems to "disappear" into your skin is the right one for you.

Above: Liquid foundations are popular.

APPLICATION KNOW-HOW

● Apply foundation to freshly moisturized skin to ensure you have a perfect base on which to work.
● Use a cosmetic sponge to apply most types of foundation – using your fingertips can result in an uneven, greasy finish.
● Apply foundation in dots, then blend each one with your sponge.
● Dampen the sponge first of all, then squeeze out the excess moisture – this will prevent the sponge from soaking up too much costly foundation.

● Check for tell-tale "tidemarks" on your jawline, nose, forehead and chin.

HIGH PERFORMANCE FOUNDATION

Companies these days have made wonderful improvements to their foundations. Here are some benefits to look out for.

● Many companies have added sunscreens to their foundations, so they'll protect you from the ageing effects of the sun while you wear them. Look out for the the words UV Protection and Sun Protection Factor (SPF) numbers on the tube or bottle.

● Look for the new "light-diffusing" foundations, which are great for older skins. They contain hundreds of tiny light-reflective particles that bounce light away from your skin – making fine lines, wrinkles and blemishes less noticeable.

COLOUR CORRECT

Colour corrective foundations can be worn under your normal foundation to alter the skin-tone. They can seem quite strange at first glance, but are, in fact, highly effective at toning down a high colour or boosting the colour of your complexion. Use them sparingly at first until you feel confident that you have achieved an effective, but subtle, result.

● Green foundation cools down rosiness and is great for those who blush easily. Princess Diana wore it under her normal foundation on her wedding day.

● Lavender foundation will brighten up a sallow complexion, and is great for when you're feeling tired.

● Apricot foundation will give a subtle glow to dull skin, and is a great beauty booster in the winter.

● White foundation gives a wonderful glow to all complexions, and is perfect for a special night out.

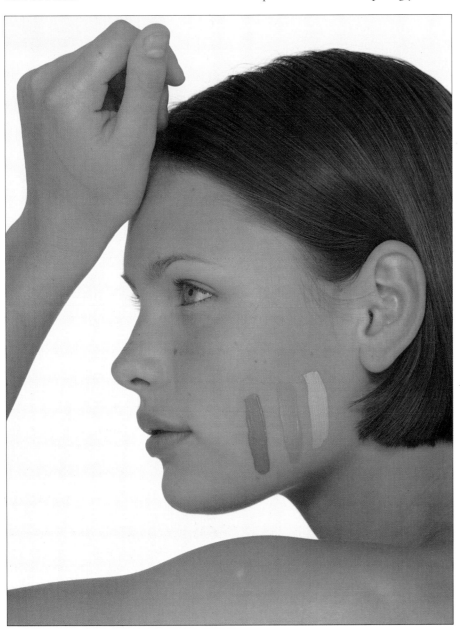

Above: Blend, blend, blend for a professional finish. And, don't forget to give all angles of your face a final check in the mirror to make sure you haven't got any unnatural lines where your foundation finishes.
Left: Before buying, check different foundation colours on your jawline for the perfect match.

CLEVER CONCEALER

Concealers are a fast and effective way to disguise blemishes, shadows, scars and red veins, so your skin looks perfect.

FIND YOUR FORMULATION

Concealers are the ideal way to cover a multitude of sins. They're a concentrated form of foundation with a very high pigment content, so they offer complete coverage to problem areas. Make-up artists argue as to whether concealer should be applied before or after foundation. I think applying it after foundation is best, as it's only applied to specific areas, and these would be disturbed when the foundation was being applied.

If you're after a light make-up effect, apply concealer directly onto clean skin, then apply powder or all-in-one foundation/powder over the top.

Stick concealers

These are easy to apply as you can simply stroke them straight onto the skin. They're the most readily available type on the market. Some have quite a heavy and thick consistency, so it's worth trying the samples in the shop before buying.

Cream concealers

These usually come in a tube, with a sponge-tipped applicator. The coverage isn't as thick as the stick type, but the finished effect is very natural.

Liquid concealers

Again, these come in a tube. Just squeeze a tiny amount of product onto your finger and smooth over the affected area. Look for the cream-to-powder formulations, which slick on like a cream and dry to a velvety powder finish.

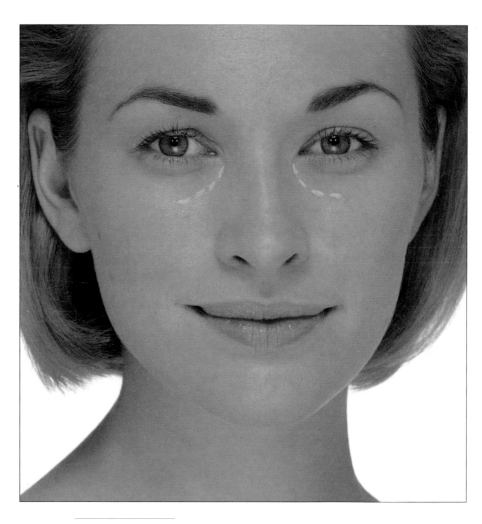

Above: Hide undereye shadows with a few dots of concealer.

> **CONCEALER TIP**
> When choosing a concealer look for the colour nearest to your own skin-tone rather than a lighter one. Covering a problem area with a paler shade will simply accentuate it.

TAKING COVER

Here's how to conceal all your beauty problems effectively.

Spots and blemishes

The ideal solution is to use a medicated stick concealer as this contains ingredients to deal with the pimple or blemish as well as cover it. Only apply the concealer exactly on the pimple or blemish, as it can be quite drying, and then smooth away the edges with a clean cotton bud (swab). Applying concealer all around the area will make the spot more noticeable and create a "halo" effect.

Under-eye shadows

Opt for a creamy stick concealer or a liquid one, as dry formulations will emphasize fine lines around your eyes. If you're blending with your fingertips, use your ring finger, as this is the weakest finger on your hand and less likely to drag at the delicate skin around your eyes.

Scars

Scars, including old acne or chickenpox marks, can be effectively covered by concealer but it can be time-consuming to get a perfect result. You need to build the indentation up to skin level by dotting on layers of concealer with a fine brush. Take your time, to allow each layer to settle into the skin properly.

Red veins

Stick or liquid concealer is ideal for this problem. Apply concealer over the area with a fine eyeliner brush or clean cotton bud (swab), then feather out the edges to stop them from being noticeable.

POW! WOW! POWDER!

Face powder is the make-up artist's best friend, as it can make your skin look really wonderful and is very versatile in its uses.

THE POWER OF POWDER

Here are four good reasons for putting on that powder!
- Powder gives a super-smooth sheen to your skin – with or without foundation.
- It "sets" your foundation, so it stays put and looks good for longer.
- Powder absorbs oils from your skin, and helps prevent shiny patches appearing.
- It helps conceal open pores.

CHOOSE YOUR POWDER

You'll need two types of powder – a loose form, and a powder compact for your handbag.

Loose powder

This gives the best and longest-lasting finish and is the choice of professional make-up artists and models. The best way to apply loose powder is to dust it lightly onto your skin using a large, soft powder brush. Then lightly brush over your face again to dust off the excess.

Pressed powder

Compacts containing pressed powder are ideal for carrying in your make-up bag as they're very quick to use and lightweight. Most come with their own application sponges, but you'll find you get a better result if you apply them with a brush. Look for brushes with retractable heads to carry in your make-up bag.

If you do use the sponge, use a light touch, and wash it regularly, or you'll transfer the oils in your skin onto the powder and get a build-up.

Shade away

Don't make the mistake of thinking that one shade of powder suits all. Instead, choose one that closely matches your skin-tone for a natural effect. Do this by dusting a little on your jawline, in the same way as you would with foundation.

Above: Powder gives a perfect featherlight finish to your skin.
Right: Choose the shade that best suits your skin colouring.

POWDER TIP
When dusting excess powder away from your skin, use your brush in light, downward strokes to help prevent the powder from getting caught in the fine hairs on your skin. Pay particular attention to the sides of the face and jawline which aren't so easy for you to see.

BEAUTIFUL BLUSHER

Give your complexion a bloom of colour with this indispensable beauty aid.

BLUSH BABY

Blusher is an instant way to give your looks a lift. It's old fashioned to use blusher to sculpt your face, as it looks so unnatural. Instead, it should be applied in the way it was first intended to be used – to recreate a youthful flush.

Powder blusher

This should be applied over the top of your foundation and face powder. To apply powder blusher, dust over the compact with a large soft brush. If you've taken too much onto your brush, tap the handle on the back of your hand to remove the excess. It's better to waste a little blusher than apply too much! A good guide is to use half as much blusher, and twice as much blending as you first think you need.

Start the colour on the fullest parts of your cheeks, directly below the centre of your eyes. Then smile and dust the blusher over your cheekbones, and up towards your temples. Blend the colour well towards the hairline, so you avoid harsh edges. This will place colour where you would naturally blush.

Right: Brush your cheeks with colour.
Below: Be a blushing beauty with a light touch of powder blusher.

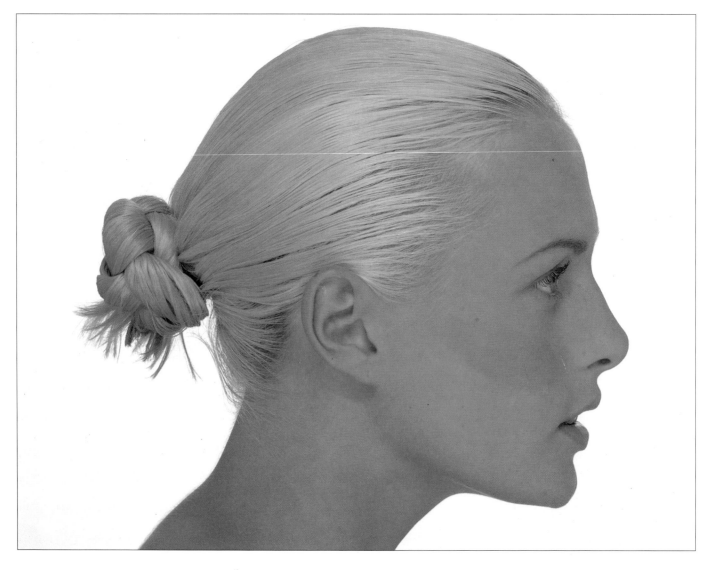

Cream blusher

Cream blusher breaks all the traditional beauty rules, as it's applied with your fingertips. It's put on after foundation, and before face powder. It's been out of fashion for some years, but has recently made a comeback. This is for good reason, as it can give a lovely fresh glow to every skin-type.

To apply, dab a few dots of cream blusher over your cheeks, from the plump part up towards your cheekbone. Using your fingertips, blend well. Build up the effect gradually, adding more blusher to create just the look you want. Or, if you prefer, you can use a foundation wedge to blend in cream blusher.

Colour choice

There's always a kaleidoscope of blusher shades to choose from. However, as a general rule, it's best to opt for a shade that tones well with your skin colouring, and co-ordinates with the rest of your make-up. You can opt for lighter or darker shades, depending on the season.

COLOUR GUIDE

Colouring	Choose
Blonde hair, cool skin	Baby pink
Blonde hair, warm skin	Tawny pink
Dark hair, cool skin	Cool rose
Dark hair, warm skin	Rosy brown
Red hair, cool skin	Soft peach
Red hair, warm skin	Warm peach
Dark hair, olive skin	Warm brown
Black hair, dark skin	Terracotta

Right: Powder blusher is a quick and easy option.
Below: Get a glow with cream blusher.

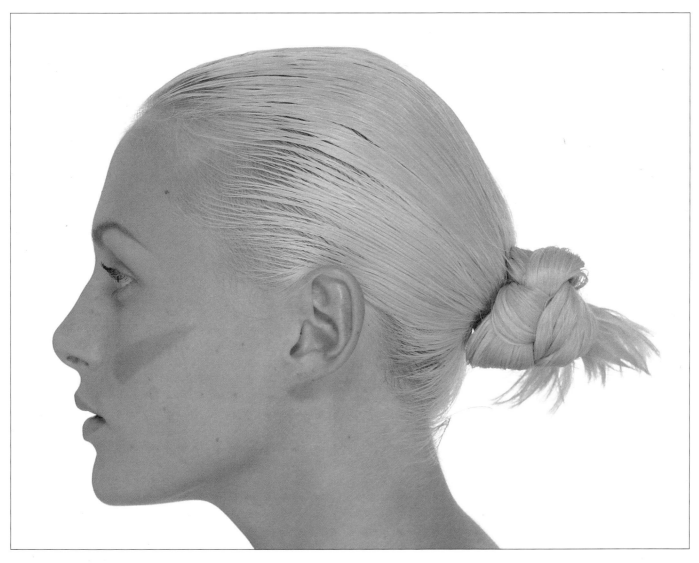

EYE-CATCHING MAKE-UP

Eye make-up is the most popular type of cosmetic, and for good reason. Just the simplest touch of mascara can open up your eyes, while a splash of colour can transform them instantly. Whatever your eye shape and colour, you can ensure they always look beautiful.

MASTERING THE BASICS

Many women hesitate to experiment with eye make-up, because it seems too time-consuming and complicated. The sheer quantity of products on the shelves and make-up counters can make it even more confusing. However, you can create a huge variety of looks – from the simplest to the most extreme – by opening your eyes to the basic techniques.

EYEBROW KNOW-HOW

Many women overlook their eyebrows, or sometimes even worse, overpluck them. When it comes to eye make-up, the eyebrows make an important impression. They can provide a balanced look to your face so it's well worth making the effort to get them looking right.

Natural brows

For perfectly groomed brows in an instant, try combing through them with a

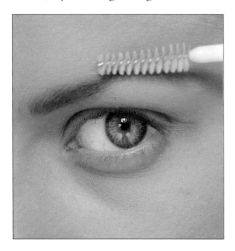

brush to flick away any powder or foundation. Comb the hairs upwards and outwards. This will also help give you a wide-eyed look. Then lightly slick them with clear gel to hold the shape in place.

Eyebrow colour

To define your brows you can use eyebrow powder or pencil. Apply powder, with an eyebrow brush, dusting it through your brows and taking care not to sweep it onto the surrounding skin.

This gives a natural effect, and requires little blending. Alternatively, use a well-sharpened pencil to draw on tiny strokes, taking care not to press too hard or the finished effect will be unnatural. Then

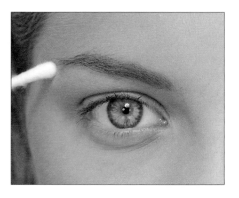

soften your the lines you've made with the eye pencil by lightly stroking a clean cotton bud (swab) through your brows.

LINING UP LINER

The different methods of eyelining change as often as fashions change. However, the basic idea of using eyeliner is a good one. Eyeliner is a great way to flatter all eye shapes and sizes. If you've never applied liner before and feel a bit nervous, try this technique.

Sit down at a table in a good light with a mirror. Take your eyeliner in your hand and rest your elbow on the table to keep your arm and hand steady. You can also give yourself extra support by resting your little finger on your cheek. Eyeliner should be applied after eyeshadow and before your mascara.

Liquid liners

These have a fluid consistency, and usually come with a brush attached to the cap. However, these aren't as easy to apply as the "ink-well" sponge-tipped variety. If you find the brush is too thick, you can pluck away hairs from it using tweezers, as this will allow you to create a thinner line. To apply the liner, look down into your mirror to prevent the liquid smudging. You should stay like this for a few seconds after applying the liner to give it time to dry thoroughly.

Pencil liners

This is the easiest way to add extra emphasis to your eyes. A pencil should be used to draw a line close to your upper and lower lashes. It's a good idea to sharpen the pencil between uses, not only to ensure you have a fine tip with which to work, but also to keep it bacteria-free.

Draw a soft line close to your lashes. If you find this quite difficult, try dotting it on along your lashes, then joining up the dots afterwards! Run over the pencil line with a brush. Alternatively, look for pencils that come with a smudger built in at the other end.

Eyeshadow as eyeliner

Make-up artists often use eyeshadow to outline the eyes, and it's a trick worth stealing! It looks great because it gives a very soft smoky effect. Use a small brush to apply shadow under your lower lashes

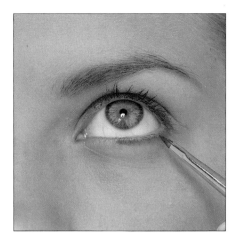

and to make an impact over the top of the eyelid, taking care to keep the shadow close to the eyelashes.

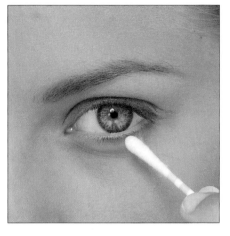

To create a softer, more modern effect simply sweep over the eyeshadow liner with a cotton bud (swab).

MASCARA MAGIC

If there's one item of make-up most women would take to a desert island, it's mascara. It's an invaluable way to create a fluttering fringe to your eyes – particularly if your lashes are fair. Most mascaras are applied with a spiral wand, as this makes them quick and easy to use. Some contain fibres to add extra length and thickness to your lashes. Opt for the waterproof variety to withstand tears, showers and swimming – but remember you'll need a suitable eye make-up remover to take it off as it clings more fiercely to your lashes than the other type.

The original block mascara is still quite popular with those who want to build up the thickness and length of their lashes gradually. Simply wet the brush with water before running the bristles over the mascara block and applying.

Applying mascara

Here are a few simple steps to perfect lashes. Start by applying mascara to your upper lashes first. Brush them downwards to start with, then brush your lashes upwards from underneath. Use a tiny zig-zag movement to prevent mascara from clogging on your lashes.

Next, use the tip of the mascara wand to brush your lower lashes, using a gentle side-to-side technique. Take care to keep your hand steady whilst you are applying the mascara, and not to blink whilst the mascara is still wet.

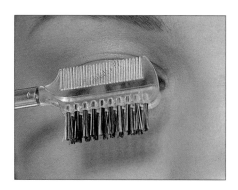

Comb through your lashes with an eyelash comb to remove any excess the wand has left behind, and to prevent your lashes from clumping together. For a more defined effect, repeat the two previous steps once or twice more, allowing each layer of mascara to dry for a few minutes before applying the next.

FALSE EYELASHES

These are great to try for party looks, although they can be tricky to apply. The strip lashes can look obvious unless you apply them perfectly. It's a better idea to use the individual lashes on the outer corners of your eyes. Dot the roots with a little glue, then use a pair of tweezers to place them exactly where you want them.

EYEING UP EYESHADOWS

Choose neutral colours to subtly enhance your looks, or play with a kaleidoscope of different shades.

Powder eyeshadows

The most popular type, these come in pressed cakes of powder either with a small brush or a sponge applicator. You can build up their density from barely-there to dramatic. Apply using a damp brush or sponge if you want a deep colour for an evening look.

Cream shadows

These are oil-based and come in little pots or compacts. They're applied either with a brush or your fingertips. They're a good choice for dry or older skins that need extra moisturizing.

Stick shadows

Wax-based, you smooth these onto your eyelids from the stick. Ensure they have a creamy texture before you buy them, so they won't drag at your skin.

Liquid shadows

Usually these come in a slim bottle with a sponge applicator. Look for the cream-to-powder ones that smooth on as a liquid and blend to a velvety powder finish.

Left: Beautiful eyes – naturally.
Below: Experiment with different coloured powder shadows.

BRUSH UP YOUR MAKE-UP

Even the most expensive make-up in the world won't look particularly great if it's applied carelessly and using your fingertips.

BASIC TOOLS

For a professional finish you need the right tools. This means investing in a set of good brushes and applicators. Here's your basic tool kit.

Make-up sponge

Have a wedge-shaped one, so you can use the finer edges to help blend in foundation round your nose and jawline, while the flatter edges are great for the cheeks, forehead and chin. However, if you prefer not to use a synthetic sponge try the small, natural ones instead.

Powder brush

Get used to using a powder brush each time you put make-up on. To prevent a caked or clogged finish to your face powder, use a large, soft brush to dust away any excess.

Blusher brush

Use to add a pretty glow to your skin with a light dusting of powder blusher. A blusher brush is slightly smaller than a powder brush to make it easier to control.

Eyeshadow brush

Smooth on any shade of eyeshadow with this brush.

Eyeshadow sponge

An sponge applicator is great for applying a sweep of pale eyeshadow that doesn't need much blending or applying highlighter to your brow bones.

All-in-one eyelash brush/comb

Great for combing through your lashes between coats of mascara for a clump-free finish. Flip the comb over and use the brush side to sweep your eyebrows into shape, or soften pencilled-in brows.

Lipbrush

Use to create a perfect outline for your lips and then use to fill in the shape with your lipstick.

Eyebrow tweezers

It is essential to have a good pair of tweezers for regularly tidying up the eyebrows.

Eyelash curlers

Once used, they'll soon become a beauty essential! Curlier eyelashes make a huge difference to the way your lashes look and help open up the eyes.

Below: Bring out the make-up artist in you with a good set of brushes.

EYE MAKE-UP MASTERCLASS

Now that you know where to start, you can experiment with more sophisticated eye make-up methods to create a variety of stunning looks. Here's a look you can try, using a wide range of techniques to create the ultimate in glamorous eye make-up.

1 Smooth over your eyelids with foundation to create an even base on which to work, and to give your eye make-up something to cling to.

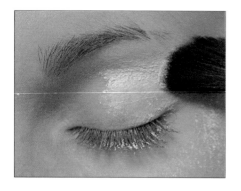

2 Sweep over your eyelids with a brush loaded with translucent face powder.

3 Dust a little translucent powder under your eyes to catch any flecks of fallen eyeshadow.

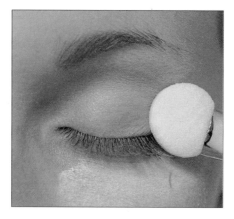

4 Use a sponge applicator to sweep a neutral ivory shade over your eyelids. Work it right up towards your eyebrows for a balanced overall effect.

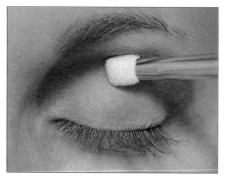

5 Smudge a brown eyeshadow into the socket line of your eyes, using a sponge applicator. If you find blending difficult, try using a slightly shimmery powder as these are easier to work in.

6 Use a brush to sweep over the top of the brown shadow as this will remove any harsh edges.

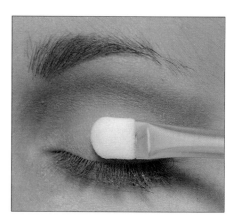

7 To create a perfectly blended finish, sweep some more ivory shadow over the edges of the brown eyeshadow using a sponge applicator.

8 Now that you've completed your eyeshadow, flick away the powder from under your eyes.

9 Looking down into a mirror and keeping your hand steady, apply liquid eyeliner along your upper lashes.

10 Use a clean cotton bud (swab) to work some brown eyeshadow under your lower lashes to add some subtle definition.

11 Squeeze your lashes with eyelash curlers to make them bend, before applying mascara. This will "open up" the eye area.

Above: For our main look here, we used a palette of ivory and blue eyeshadow, combined with black eyeliner and mascara. Take time to experiment with different colours to find a look that suits you and your colouring.

12 Apply mascara onto your upper lashes and use the tip of the mascara wand to coat your lower lashes.

13 Stroke your eyebrows with pencil to shape them and fill in any patches.

14 Smooth over the top with a cotton bud (swab) to soften the eyebrow pencil line.

LIP SERVICE

Lipstick has been around for about 5,000 years, and women have always loved it. Indeed, during the cosmetic shortages of the Second World War, British women said that lipstick was the item of make-up they missed the most. It's the easiest and quickest way to give your face a focus and give it an instant splash of colour.

A LICK OF COLOUR

Lipsticks in a bullet form are the most popular way to use lip colour. The more pigment a lipstick has, the longer it'll last on your lips. The best way to apply lipstick is with a lipbrush.

Above: A slick of colour will make you love your lips.
Right: A selection of lipstick colours is the key to creating different looks.

Another way of applying colour is with a lip gloss. These can be used alone to give your lips an attractive sheen, or over the top of lipstick to catch the light.

Lip liners are used to provide an outline to your lips before applying lipstick. You can also use them over your entire lip for a dark, matte effect. However, you may need to add a touch of lipsalve (balm) over the top to prevent drying out this delicate area of skin.

STEP-BY-STEP TO PERFECT LIPS

SPECIAL INGREDIENTS

Today's lipsticks offer more than just a pigment to give your lips colour. In just the same way as technology has been used in skin-care products, lipsticks often contain other ingredients to care for the delicate skin on your lips. Here are some that may be included in your lipstick.

● Vegetable wax to make your lipstick smooth on easily, and give a lovely sheen.
● Liposomes containing active moisturizing ingredients, to keep your lips soft.
● Chamomile to soothe and heal the skin on your lips.
● Shea butter to deep-moisturize your lips, especially in extremes of weather and

the wind, which can have drastic effects.
● Silica to help give your lipstick a slightly matte effect.
● UV filters to protect your lips against the ageing effects of the sun's rays.
● Vitamin E to heal any cuts, and to protect your lips against the fine lines associated with ageing.

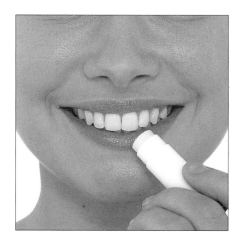

1 Ensure your lips are soft and supple by smoothing over some lipsalve (balm) before you start.

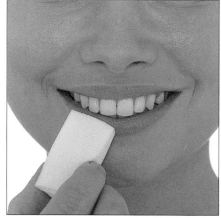

2 Prime your lips by smoothing them with foundation, using a make-up sponge so you reach every tiny crevice on the surface.

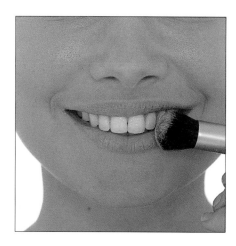

3 Dust over the top of the foundation with a light dusting of your usual face powder, to ensure your lipstick will stay put for longer.

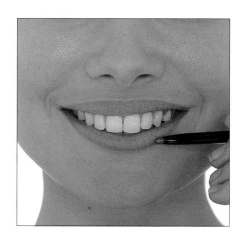

4 Rest your elbow on a firm surface and carefully draw an outline using a lip pencil. So it doesn't drag your skin, it may help to warm it slightly in your palm. Start by defining the Cupid's bow on the upper lip, then draw a neat outline on your lower lip. Finish by completing the edges of the outline to your upper lip.

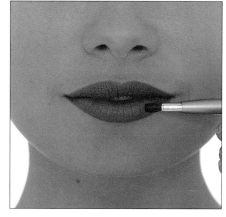

5 Use a lipbrush to fill in the outline with lipstick, ensuring you reach into every tiny crevice on the surface. Open your mouth to brush the colour into the corners of your lips.

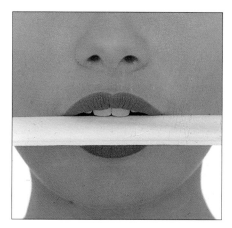

6 You'll make your lipstick last longer if you blot over the surface with a tissue. It'll also give an attractive, semi-matte finish to your lips.

COOL SKIN, BLONDE HAIR

With your porcelain complexion and pale hair, you should opt for baby pastel tones with sheer formulations and a hint of shimmer. This way you'll flatter your colouring with a light, fresh make-up look, without overpowering it.

THIS LOOK SUITS YOU IF...

- You have pale blonde to mousey or mid-blonde hair. It also suits women with white hair or steel-grey hair.
- Your eyes are blue, grey, hazel or green.
- You have pale skin, including whiter-than-white, ivory or a pinky "English rose" complexion.

TIPS
- If you're over 35, or unsure about wearing blue eyeshadow, swap it for a cool grey shade. This will create the same soft effect, but it's slightly more subtle.
- Shimmery eyeshadow can highlight crepey eyelids, so you may prefer to switch to a matte ivory shadow instead.

1 Your delicate skin doesn't need heavy coverage, so use a light tinted moisturizer. Dot it lightly onto your nose, cheeks, forehead and chin, then blend it in with your fingertips.

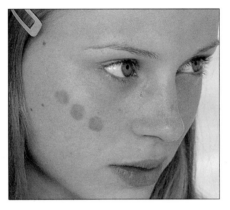

2 Cool pink, cream blusher will give a soft glow to your skin. Dot onto your cheeks, then blend in with your fingertips. You can either skip powder to leave your skin with a dewy glow, or dust a little over your face. However, use a gentle touch, as you want to let your natural skin-tone shine through.

3 Take a baby blue eyeshadow onto an eyeshadow brush and sweep it evenly over your entire eyelid. Stroke the brush gently over your eyelid a few times until you've swept away any obvious edges to the eyeshadow. Also work a little colour under your lower lashes.

4 Sweep a shimmery ivory shadow from the crease of your eyelid up towards the brow bone. Finish with two coats of brown/black mascara.

5 Stroke your eyebrows into shape with an eyebrow brush. This will also flick away any powder that's got caught in the hairs.

6 Cool pink lipstick should be applied with a lipbrush. If you like, you can slick a little lipgloss or lip balm on top for a sexy shimmer.

WARM SKIN, BLONDE HAIR

Although you have a warm skin-tone, your overall look is quite delicate. This means you should opt for tawny, neutral shades of make-up, and apply them with a light touch so you enhance your basic colouring.

THIS LOOK SUITS YOU IF...

● You have golden, warm blonde or dark blonde hair. This look also suits women with greying hair that has warm or yellow undertones.

● Your eyes are brown, blue, hazel or green – it will work equally well.

● You have a warm skin-tone which can develop a light, golden tan.

● Your skin tone and blonde hair mean your overall look is quite delicate. If so, you need to choose make-up shades that are not too intense, like those here.

1 After applying a light, tinted moisturizer, stroke concealer onto problem areas. Blondes tend to have fine skin, often prone to surface thread veins. Cover these effectively with concealer, applied with a clean cotton bud (swab).

2 Dip a powder puff into loose powder and lightly press over the areas of your face that are prone to oiliness. This will absorb excess oil throughout the day, and leave your skin beautifully matte. Dust off any excess powder with a clean powder brush.

3 Sweep peach eyeshadow over your entire eyelid. It will blend with your natural skin-tone, but give a clean, wide-eyed look to your make-up.

4 Use an eyeshadow brush to work a tiny amount of soft brown eyeshadow into the crease of your eyelid to create depth and definition to your eyes. Sweep it out towards the outer corner of your eyes as well.

5 Still using the same brown eyeshadow, work a little underneath your lower lashes. This gives a softer effect than traditional kohl pencil or eyeliner, and is particularly suitable for those with pale or blonde hair who often can't carry off very strong eye make-up. Finish with two coats of brown/black mascara.

6 Apply a barely-there shade of nude lipstick with a lipbrush. Then apply your tawny blusher, sweeping it a little at a time over your cheeks, forehead, and chin. You can even dust a little over the tip of your nose! The advantage of applying blusher after you've completed your make-up is that you can assess exactly how much you need.

COOL SKIN, DARK HAIR

Pale-skinned brunettes look fabulous with strong, cool shades of cosmetics. The density of colour provides a striking contrast to ivory skin-tones, while their coolness tones in beautifully with your natural beauty.

THIS LOOK SUITS YOU IF...

● You have medium brown to dark brown hair.

● Your eyes are brown, blue, hazel, grey or green.

● You have a cool, China doll skin-tone, that tans slowly in the sun.

Tips

● To stop your mascara from clogging wiggle the mascara wand from side to side as you pull it through your lashes.

● If you find cream blusher hard to apply you can opt for the powder variety, applying it after face powder.

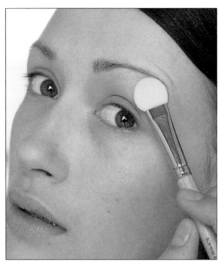

1 Apply foundation or tinted moisturizer. If using foundation, it's likely you'll need the palest of shades. Blend in a few dots of tawny cream blusher. Finish with a dusting of loose powder.

2 Smudge a cool ivory shadow over your eyelids, right up to your eyebrows. Stroke over it with a cotton bud (swab) to blend it if you find it gathers in creases close to your upper eyelashes.

3 Add extra definition with a touch of taupe or khaki eyeshadow on your eyelids. This shade works beautifully on your cool colouring, and emphasizes the colour of your eyes really well.

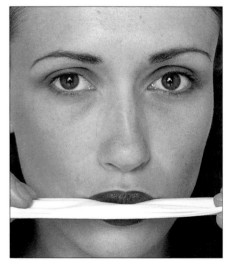

4 Now move onto your eyelashes. You need to apply two thin coats of black mascara to create a wonderful frame to your eyes.

5 Slick your eyebrows into place with an eyebrow brush. If they tend to look untidy, hold them in place by spritzing the brush with a little hairspray first.

6 Choose a clear shade of berry lipstick to give your look a polished finish. Blot after one coat with a tissue, then re-apply for a longer-lasting finish.

WARM SKIN, DARK HAIR

Your skin-tone can carry off burnished browns, warm reds and earthy shades beautifully. They'll complement your complexion and emphasize your features.

THIS LOOK SUITS YOU IF...

- You have mid to dark brown hair.
- Your eyes are brown, dark blue, grey, hazel or green.
- You have a warm skin-tone that usually tans quite well. Even if it is pale in winter, your skin still has a yellow undertone.

1 Dot liquid foundation onto your skin and blend in with a damp cosmetic sponge. Blend the colour into your neckline for a natural effect. Then apply concealer to any blemishes that need them.

2 Pat your face with translucent loose powder, then fluff off the excess with a large, soft brush.

3 Use a sponge-tipped eyeshadow applicator to sweep a red-brown shadow over your entire eyelid. The advantage of the sponge over a brush is that it doesn't tend to flick colour around. Complete your eyes with two thin coats of mascara.

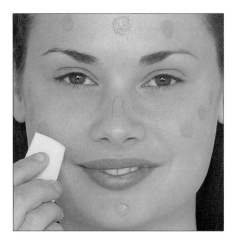

4 Your eyebrows need subtle emphasis for this look. Either pencil them in with soft strokes of brown eyebrow pencil, or use a brown eyeshadow for a softer effect. Whichever method you use, brush them with an eyebrow brush to blend the strokes and slick the hairs in place.

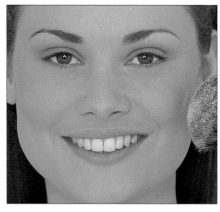

5 Opt for a warm, tawny brown shade of powder blusher, dusted over your cheeks and up towards your temples. As this colour is quite strong, you may need to tone it down a little afterwards by dusting lightly over the top with translucent loose powder.

6 A fiery red lipstick balances the overall look. Use a lipbrush to ensure you fill in every tiny crease and crevice on the lip surface – this will help your lipstick colour stay put for longer as well as create a perfect finish.

COOL SKIN, RED HAIR

Redheads with cool skin-tones often stick to wishy-washy colours, but you can experiment with brighter colours to contrast with your wonderful colouring. Greens give an exciting dimension to your eyes, and strong earthy shades supercharge your lips.

THIS LOOK SUITS YOU IF...

● You have strawberry-blonde or pale red hair, even if the colour has faded.
● Your eyes are blue, grey, hazel or green.
● You have pale skin, ranging from ivory to a pink-toned complexion.

Tip
If you've got freckles, don't fall into the trap of trying to cover them with a dark-toned foundation. Instead, match your foundation to your skin-tone to avoid a mask-like effect.

1 Apply foundation and concealer, then dot a peachy shade of cream blusher onto your cheekbones. Unlike powder blusher, you can blend the cream variety with your fingertips – as the warmth from your skin will help smooth it in evenly. Apply a little cream blusher at a time. Finish with a dusting of translucent powder.

2 A neutral, peach-toned eyeshadow swept over your eyelids will emphasize your eye colour without fighting with it. Ensure you take care to work it close to your eyelashes, to create a balanced effect.

3 Redheads usually have fair eyebrows, so don't forget to emphasize them to create a frame to your eyes. Otherwise the rest of your make-up will look unbalanced as the focus will be placed on your forehead. Opt for a very pale eyebrow pencil, in a subtle grey-brown tone. Stroke it through your eyebrows, taking care to fill any bald spots. Then soften the lines by brushing through with an eyebrow comb.

4 Brush a hint of gold, shimmery eyeshadow into the arch under your eyebrows to give your eyes an extra dimension and bring them subtly into focus. This is a particularly good way to bring out gold flecks or warmth in the iris of your eyes.

5 Green eyeliner looks wonderful on your eyes and colouring! Don't fall into the trap of just smudging it under your lower lashes as this will drag your features downwards. Instead, work it along your upper lashes and into the corners of your eyes as well. Once you've applied it, smudge over the top with a clean cotton bud (swab) to give a softer finish. It's also a good idea to brush a little translucent powder over the top to ensure it stays put. Complete your eyes with two good coats of brown mascara.

6 Burnished orange lipstick complements this look. Begin by outlining your lips with a toning lip liner to prevent the colour from bleeding. Then use a lipbrush to fill in with the lipstick.

WARM SKIN, RED HAIR

Your vibrant Pre-Raphaelite colouring is suited to bold shades of wine, purple and brown. These deep, blue-toned colours look fabulous with your warm skin and hair tones, and can make you look truly stunning.

THIS LOOK SUITS YOU IF...

- You have medium to dark red hair. This look may also suit brunettes who have a lot of red tones to their hair.
- Your eyes are blue, grey, hazel, brown or green.

- You have a medium to warm skin-tone.
- Your skin takes on a golden colour in the summer, although you're unlikely to get a deep tan. It's quite likely that you have freckles.

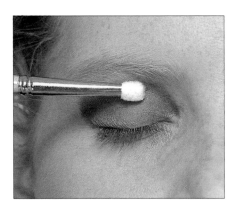

1 After applying foundation, concealer and powder, smooth a wine shade of shadow over your entire eyelid. Using a sponge-tipped eyeshadow applicator will give you more control when applying this colour. You may find it easier to blend in if you sweep some translucent powder over your eyelids first, to create a smooth base on which to work.

2 Use a pale mauve eyeshadow over your brow bone to balance your eye make-up. Blend it into the crease, to soften any harsh edges of the wine-toned eyeshadow. Take the time at this stage, for a professional-looking finish.

3 Smudge a little of the wine-toned eyeshadow under your lower lashes as well. This will give a modern look to your eye make-up, and give a softer effect than kohl pencil. Ensure you also work it into the outer corners of your eyes, sweeping it slightly upwards to give your eyes a lift. Then finish with two coats of brown mascara. Take care to take the mascara right to the roots of your lashes, especially if they're pale.

4 Use a soft brown eyeshadow on your eyebrows to give them subtle emphasis, using either a small brush, or a cotton bud (swab). Brush the eyebrows through afterwards with an eyebrow comb for a soft finish.

5 Choose a brown-toned blusher or bronzing powder to give your skin lots of warmth. Dust it on with a large blusher brush, blending it out towards your hairline for a natural glow. The key is to use a little at a time, increasing the intensity of colour as you go. It's best to avoid shimmery blushers, as these can sometimes give your skin a rather unnatural looking sheen.

6 You can carry off a deep plum shade of lipstick, outlined with a toning lip pencil. This strong colour needs perfect application to look good, so apply two coats, blotting in between with a tissue. This will also ensure your lipstick stays put for ages, and avoids the need for constant retouching.

OLIVE SKIN, DARK HAIR

Your skin-tones are easy to complement with rich browns, oranges and a hint of gold or bronze. These rich shades define your features and work well on your wonderful skin-tones.

THIS LOOK SUITS YOU IF...

● You have dark brown to black hair.
● Your eyes are brown, hazel or green.
● Your olive skin tans beautifully, or you have Asian or Indian colouring.

TIP
To create a perfect lip line, stretch your mouth into an "O" shape and fill in the corners with your lip pencil.

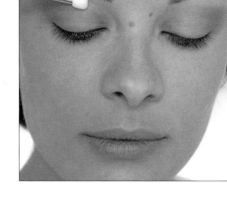

1 Even out minor skin blemishes with a tinted moisturizer, blending it in with fingertips. If you need more coverage, opt for a liquid or cream foundation. Now apply a concealer and a light dusting of face powder.

2 After sweeping a golden shade of shadow across your entire eyelid, apply a darker bronze shade into the crease and then apply some under the lower lashes. This gives a wonderfully sultry look to your eyes.

3 Take a warm brown eyeliner, and work it along your upper and lower lashes for a strong look that you can carry off beautifully. If you find the effect too harsh, smudge with a clean cotton bud (swab). Apply two coats of black mascara.

4 A peach-brown powder blusher adds a sunkissed warmth to your cheeks. Apply just a little at a time, increasing the effect as you go.

5 Outline your lips with an orange-brown lip pencil. Start at the Cupid's bow on the upper lip, and move outwards. Then complete the other side, and finish with the lower lip.

6 To complete the look fill in with a sunny orange shade of lipstick. If you like a glamorous, glossy finish, don't blot your lips with a tissue You can even add a dab of lip balm for extra shine if you wish. But if you like a semi-matte look, blot after one coat with a tissue, then re-apply your lipstick for a longer-lasting finish.

OLIVE SKIN, ORIENTAL COLOURING

Your black hair, and pale – but yellow-toned – skin are best complemented by soft, warm colours. These will define your looks and counteract any sallowness in your complexion.

THIS LOOK SUITS YOU IF...

● You have very dark brown to blue-black hair. It also works if you have grey flecks in your hair.
● Your eyes are hazel or brown.
● You have a pale to medium skin-tone. It does tan, although it has a tendency to look quite yellow.

TIP
Oriental eyelashes are often poker-straight and so you can really benefit from the use of eyelash curlers.

1 After applying foundation, concealer and powder, sweep some lilac eyeshadow over your eyelid. This pale colour is a better option than using darker eyeshadows near the eyes as they have a tendency to make them look deep-set, particularly as your eyelids tend to be quite small.

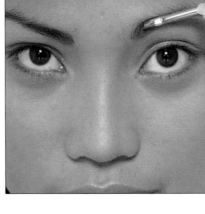

2 Lightly fill in your eyebrows with a dark brown eyeshadow or eyebrow pencil to provide a strong frame to your eyes. This will help balance the eyeliner which is going to be applied next.

3 A lick of blue-black eyeliner will emphasize your beautifully-shaped eyes, and help correct any droopiness. Slick it along the lower lashes and into the outer corners of your eyes to create balance. To prevent the overall look from seeming too harsh, use a cotton bud (swab) to soften the eyeliner slightly.

4 Place your eyelashes between the edges of a curler, and gently squeeze for a few seconds. Then apply two coats of black mascara.

5 A warm pink blusher gives a wonderful boost to your complexion, and brings out its natural glow. Dust it over the plumpest part of your cheeks.

6 A baby pink lipliner and lipstick bring your lips fashionably into focus. The cool blue-tone to this shade works wonderfully on your colouring.

BLACK HAIR, PALE BLACK SKIN

Try emphasizing your looks with earthy shades. Your gold or red-toned skin works wonderfully with beige, brown and copper colours.

THIS LOOK SUITS YOU IF...

● You have black hair with golden or reddish highlights. It also works if you have grey flecks in your hair.
● You have hazel or brown eyes.
● You have a black skin.

1 After applying foundation, dust on a translucent face powder, ensuring it perfectly matches your skin-tone to avoid a chalky looking complexion. Dust off the excess with a large powder brush, using downward strokes.

2 Use an eyeshadow brush to dust an ivory-toned eyeshadow over your entire eyelid, to create a contrast with your warm skin-tone.

3 Smudge a deep-toned brown eye-shadow into the crease of your eye-lid, blending it thoroughly. Also work a little of this colour into the outer corners, and underneath your lower lashes to make your eyes look really striking.

4 Black liquid eyeliner swept along your upper lashes will give a super-model look to your eyes. A sponge-tipped applicator is easier to use than a brush. Apply the eyeliner whilst looking down into a mirror, as this stretches any creases out of your eyelid. Rest your elbow on a firm surface. Complete your eyes with two coats of black mascara.

5 Use a brown lipliner pencil to out-line your lips. You can use an ordi-nary brown eyeliner pencil if this is the only thing you have to hand. Blend the line lightly into your lips, using a cotton bud (swab) for a softer effect.

6 A neutral pink-brown lipstick gives a natural looking sheen to your lips, and instantly updates your looks. Apply it with a lipbrush for an even finish.

BLACK HAIR, DEEP BLACK SKIN

You can experiment with endless colour possibilities as your dark eyes, hair and skin provide the perfect canvas on which to work. The key to success is to choose bold, deep colours as your skin demands these to achieve a wonderful glow.

THIS LOOK SUITS YOU IF...

● You have deep black hair, even if it has flecks of grey.
● You have dark hazel or brown eyes.
● You have a dark black skin.

TIP
While dramatic colours suit your skin-tone and colouring perfectly, be sure to apply them with a light touch to get a fresh, up-to-date look.

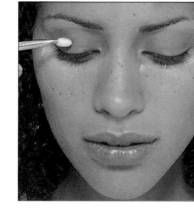

1 Take care to find a foundation that matches your skin-tone exactly. Apply it with a sponge so it blends in perfectly. Dampen the sponge with water first to give it extra "slip", and to prevent the sponge from absorbing too much pricey foundation. Blend in thoroughly along your jaw and hairline to avoid tide-marks. Finally, set with a light dusting of translucent loose powder.

2 Next, sweep a dark blackcurrant eyeshadow over your eyelids. Dust a little loose powder under your eyes first to catch any falling specks of this dark shade, and prevent it from ruining your completed foundation.

3 Apply a dark charcoal eyeshadow into the crease of your eyelid, using an eyeshadow brush. Only take a little colour at a time onto the brush to prevent it from spilling onto your eyelid. If necessary, tap the brush on the back of your hand first to shake away any excess.

4 Use an eyeliner brush to work some of this charcoal shade under your lower lashes – as this is the ideal colour to outline your eyes with. Hold the mirror slightly above your eyeliner so you can achieve an accurate liner effect. Finish with two coats of black mascara.

5 A tawny brown shade of blusher complements your skin beautifully. With a large round brush, dust it over the apple of your cheeks, working it lightly out towards your hairline.

6 After outlining your lips with a toning lip pencil, fill in with a dark plum shade of lipstick, using a lipbrush.

TAKE FIVE FOR NIGHT-TIME GLAMOUR

When you haven't got time to spare, but want to look presentable, try this quick routine for evening sophistication. This isn't the time to experiment with new ideas, so the key is to choose simple looks, applied with minimum of fuss when you're racing the clock... in other words, simple steps to a sexy look!

Five minutes to go...

The all-in-one foundation/powder formulations give your skin the medium coverage it needs for this look in half the normal time. Also, take it over your lips and eyelids as this will make the rest of your make-up easier to apply and ensure it lasts the whole evening.

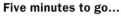

Four minutes to go...

Cream eyeshadow applied straight from the stick is quick and easy to apply. Opt for a brown shade as it'll bring out the colour of your eyes, and give them a sexy, sultry finish. Slick it over your entire eyelid, right up to the crease of the eye socket.

Three and a half minutes to go...

A swift way to blend in your eyeshadow is to brush over the top with translucent loose powder. This will tone down the colour and blend away any harsh edges.

Two and a half minutes to go...

Apply a coat of mascara to your lashes, taking care to colour your lower lashes as well as your upper ones. Use the tip of the mascara wand to coat the lower lashes, as this will prevent it from clogging on the hairs – and prevent you from spending valuable time having to use an eyelash comb.

One and a half minutes to go...

A warm berry red blusher will give your skin a fabulous flush. Apply it with a blusher brush, sweeping it from your cheeks up towards your eyes to give your face a lift.

Thirty seconds to go...

Choose a berry shade of lip gloss to add instant bold colour to your lips, sweeping it straight on with the sponge-tipped applicator. Cover your lower lip first, then press your lips together to transfer some of the colour onto your upper lip. Touch up any areas you've missed with the applicator, and you're ready to go!

Right: Six quick steps to a sexy look.

MAKE-UP TO LOOK YOUNGER!

If you haven't changed your make-up in years, it's a fair bet you're not making the most of your looks. Wearing out-of-fashion make-up is a sure way to add years to your appearance. Our simple make-up rules will help you break out of a beauty rut.

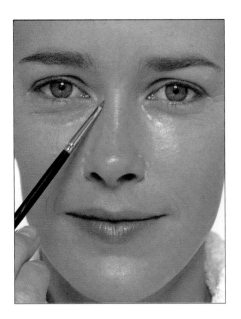

Simple steps to perfect skin
A dull, lifeless skin-tone can make you look, and feel, drab. The great news is, there are now foundations and concealers on the market specially designed to deal with this problem. Basically, the formulations contain hundreds of light-reflective particles and these bounce light away from your skin. This gives your skin the illusion of added vitality, and helps disguise problem areas such as fine lines and under-eye shadows.

And, the great news is that these light-reflective foundations and concealers are not just limited to expensive prestige beauty counters – these days, the price-conscious companies offer them too.

Apply your foundation with a damp sponge, blending away any harsh edges to avoid tell-tale tidemarks. This is the stage to apply concealer, dotting it onto under-eye shadows, blemishes and thread veins with a brush. Apply a tiny amount at a time, and blend thoroughly.

BEFORE YOU START
Avoid extremes of fashion and bright colours when you're over 40. While younger skins can just about get away with garish make-up, it'll simply emphasize fine lines and wrinkles on most women. Concentrate instead on flattering your looks with subtle colours. So, throw away those traffic-stopping blue eyeshadows and neon lipsticks!

Add a youthful glow with blusher
Forget about adding colour to your skin with foundation – you'll be left with a mask effect, and "tidemarks" on your jawline. Instead, recreate a youthful bloom with a light touch of blusher. Remember though, to use half as much blusher and twice as much blending as you originally think! The cream variety of blusher is a good one to try, because it will give your skin a soft glow. Dot the blusher onto your skin, and blend with your fingertips.

Lightly set your foundation and blusher with translucent powder. A common mistake among many women is to be heavy-handed with face powder. Applying too much can make it settle into fine lines and wrinkles on your face, and emphasize them. Aim for a light touch, which will just blot out shine and set your make-up.

The best way to apply powder is only to blot the areas that need it, then brush away the excess with a large powder brush, stroking the brush downwards to prevent tiny particles catching in the fine hairs on your face.

If you haven't got a clue where to start, make an appointment for a free makeover at a local beauty counter. This way you'll be able to see which shades suit you, before you launch out and buy.

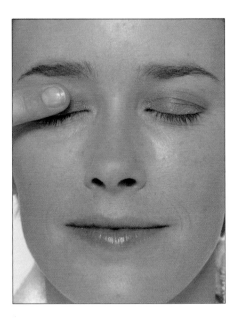

Be subtle with eyeshadow
Lots of women never perfect the technique of applying eyeshadow properly. Thankfully, now there's a new type of eyeshadow formulation that is a cinch to apply - cream-to-powder eyeshadow. It applies as a smooth cream, and dries quickly to a super-soft powder finish. Opt for a subtle shade, such as mid-brown, grey or taupe.

A good tip if your eyes look rather droopy is to blend eyeshadow upwards and outwards at the outer corners. Remember to blend it in well.

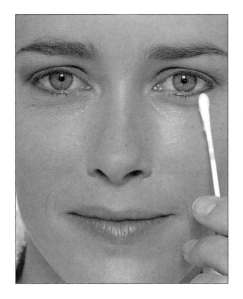

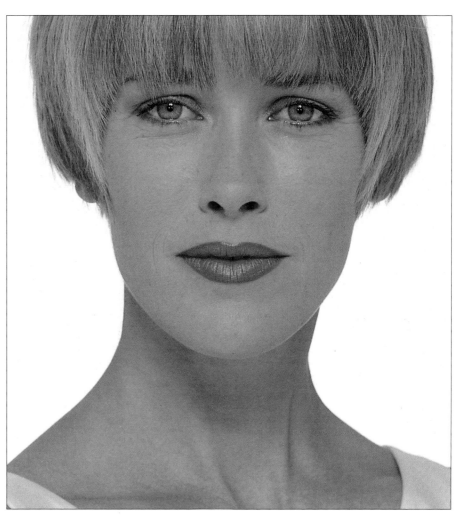

Give eyeliners a miss

Harsh lines of colour close to your eyes can be hard and unflattering. You'll emphasize your eyes much better if you smudge a little neutral-toned powder eyeshadow under your lower lashes with a clean cotton bud (swab).

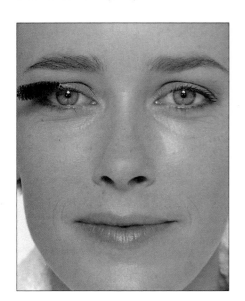

Above: Follow these six simple ideas to help you break out of a beauty rut.

Check your mascara colour

Most women's colouring fades slightly over the years. This means that the black mascara you're used to wearing can now look too obvious and harsh. So, try switching to a lighter shade for a more flattering effect. Apply two thin coats, allowing time for the first to dry thoroughly before you apply the second one.

Recreate your lip line

If your lip line has started to fade, and your lipstick tends to "bleed" into the lines around your mouth, try using a toning lipliner before you apply lipstick. Check it's firm enough to give a precise line, yet soft enough not to drag your skin. Apply by outlining your top lip first, working from the Cupid's bow outwards to each corner. Then outline your lower lip. Next dust your lips with loose powder to set the lipliner.

Finally, fill in your outline with a moisturizing lipstick. This will also help give a glossy shine to your lips which makes them look fuller. Apply with a lipbrush, blot with a tissue, then reapply for a longer-lasting finish.

CLASSIC CHIC

Whatever your age or colouring, this simple but highly effective classic look will always make a pleasing impact!

1 Apply a sheer all-in-one foundation-powder. This will give your skin the perfect coverage it needs to carry off strong lips, without clogging up your skin. Thick foundation is very much out of fashion these days. Natural-looking skin is much more attractive.

2 The eye make-up for this look is very understated. So, use an eyelash curler to open up your eyes and give them a fresh look.

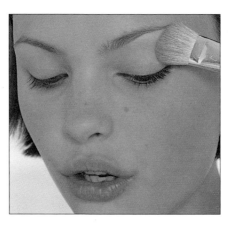

3 Sweep some pale ivory eyeshadow across your entire eyelid using a blender brush. Then complete your eyes with two thin coats of brown-black or black mascara.

4 Well-groomed eyebrows are essential. Brush them against the growth to remove any stray flecks of powder or foundation. Then lightly fill in any gaps with a toning eyeshadow. This gives a softer, more natural effect than pencil.

COLOUR CODING

Believe it or not, everyone can wear red lipstick. The key to success is to choose just the right shade for your colouring.

Colouring	Choose
Blonde hair, cool skin	If you're daring enough your can wear any bright red shade, such as crimson or fire engine red. Any bold shade will look really effective and striking on you.
Blonde hair, warm skin	Lovely pink-reds look wonderful with your colouring. They're delicate enough not to look too harsh, while the pinky undertones complement the warmth of your skin.
Dark hair, cool skin	Rich blue reds, such as wine, burgundy and blood-red look wonderful on your China doll features. The contrast of dark hair, pale skin and red lips is really stunning!
Dark hair, warm skin	Rich brick reds and ruby jewel-like shades. Their warmth is very flattering to your complexion, while the intensity of colour looks great against your hair.
Red hair, cool skin	Choose a delicate orange-red, a paler version of the one mentioned above. This will add a wonderful splash of colour without overpowering you.
Red hair, warm skin	Warm, fiery reds with brown undertones, to complement your rich hair colour and rosy skin.
Dark hair, olive skin	Rich red, with orange undertones will flatter your skin. Go for a bold colour, as you can carry it off.
Black hair, brown skin	Berry reds and burgundy reds look wonderful on your skin.

5 Your lips are the focus of this chic look. To ensure that you create a perfect outline, use a toning red lip pencil. Rest your elbow on a hard surface when using the pencil to prevent your hand from wobbling.

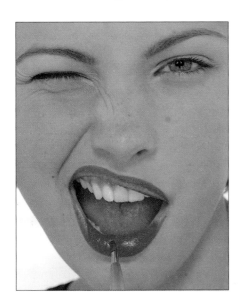

6 Use a lipbrush to fill in with a bold shade of red lipstick. Apply one coat, blot with a tissue, then reapply for a long-lasting finish.

Right: Make-up trends come and go, but red lipstick is always in fashion!

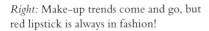

COUNTRY GIRL MAKE-UP

If you want a fresh, outdoor look, try this summery make-up – complete with fake freckles!

1 You need to avoid heavy foundations when you're outside, so tinted moisturizer is the perfect solution. It'll both nourish your skin and lightly cover any minor blemishes. Apply with your fingertips for ease.

2 If you already have freckles, don't try to hide them – they're perfect for a fresh-air look. If you don't have them, then fake them! Use an eyebrow pencil rather than an eyeliner pencil as it has a harder consistency and is less likely to melt on the skin. Use a mid-brown shade, and dot on the freckles, concentrating them on the nose and cheeks. Be extra creative, and apply different sizes of freckles for a realistic look.

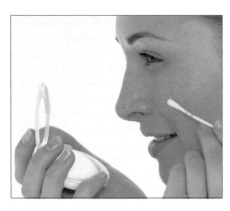

3 To make your faux freckles look real, soften the edges with a clean cotton bud (swab). Then dust your skin with loose powder to set them in place.

4 A bronzing powder rather than a blusher will give your skin a sunkissed outdoor look. Choose one with minimum pearl or shimmer. Apply it to the plumpest part of your cheeks, where the sun would naturally catch your face. Dust the bronzing powder over your temples, too.

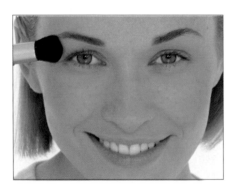

5 Swap to an eyeshadow blending brush to sweep some of the bronzing powder over your eyelids. Natural colours like brown work best for this look. Remove any harsh edges with a clean cotton bud (swab).

6 Keep mascara to a minimum. Choose a natural-looking brown or brown/black shade, and apply just one coat. The waterproof type is great for hot days and sudden downpours but remember you'll need a waterproof eye make-up remover, too.

7 Don't overpower the look with bold lipstick. Opt for a muted brown-pink shade that's close to your natural lipcolour or use a tinted lipgloss for a natural sheen.

Right: A light, fresh, outdoor look.

CITY CHIC MAKE-UP

This super-successful look is great for work and in the city. Simple, perfectly applied colours can help you put together a polished working image. This stylish, balanced look will make you feel really confident and will leave you to ready to get on with the more important things in your day!

1 After applying a light foundation, and dusting your skin with powder to blot out shine, sweep your eyelids with a mid-grey eyeshadow. Use a matte powder formulation as this doesn't tend to crease as much during the day. Use a sponge-tipped applicator to make the eyeshadow easier to apply.

2 Use a beige highlighting eyeshadow over your brow bone to soften the edges of the grey shadow and to bring

your eyes into focus. Take care not to leave flecks of powder in your eyebrow hairs – if necessary, flick them away with an eyebrow brush. Finish with two coats of mascara – blondes should use brown or brown-black mascara, while other colourings can opt for black.

3 Brush your eyebrows with brown eyeshadow to fill in any gaps. This helps to create a strong frame to your make-up look.

4 A soft pink shade of blusher will give your skin a rosy glow, and coordinate the rest of your make-up. And, it will give pale work-a-day faces an immediate lift!

5 Try soft blackcurrant shades as these can work beautifully on your lips, and make a welcome alternative to red lips. Start by using a lipliner to outline, ensuring you take it well into the outer corners. If you create any wobbly edges, whisk over the top with a clean cotton bud (swab) dipped in a little cleansing lotion. Then re-powder and try again!

6 Fill in your lips with a matching shade of blackcurrant lipstick. Blot your lips with a tissue afterwards for a semi-matte finish that's perfect for a day at the office.

WORKING WOMAN BASICS

You need to bear some simple pointers in mind to ensure you look good right through from 9 'til 5 – and beyond! Here are some tips to bear in mind.

● Choose a clear, plastic make-up bag so you can find what you're looking for in an instant – it saves rummaging around!

● Buy a make-up mirror in its own case, so it's always dust and make-up free. Powder compacts tend to become covered by the make-up inside, and are usually too small to be particularly effective.

● Look out for retractable powder and lipbrushes, so you can simply twist them up and they're ready to use. It's unhygienic to use a brush which has bristles that are gathering dust and grime in the bottom of your make-up bag.

● Also carry a nail file for emergency tears or splits, and a small hairbrush and travel-size hairspray to keep your hair looking preened and polished, too.

Below: Clever make-up moves for a smart 9 'til 5 look.

GO FOR GLAMOUR!

If there's one time you want to make a special effort with your make-up and pull out all the stops, it's a big night out! We'll show you how to create this stunning look, which combines a mixture of dark and light tones.

and provide a smooth base on which to apply your eyeliner at the next stage. The emphasis is on glamour and impact!

Tip
Wind your hair round velcro rollers while applying your make-up. Then, all you do is remove them, run your fingers through your hair and you're ready to party!

1 This is a sophisticated look, with the focus very much on the eyes. Once you've applied foundation, concealer and powder, you're ready to start work on your eye make-up. Sweep a smoky dark brown eyeshadow over your entire eyelid and blend it carefully into the crease. A simple sponge applicator is less likely to flick colour away than a brush, but still take the precaution of sweeping a line of loose powder under your eyes to catch any falling specks of dark shadow.

3 Whereas black eyeliner is usually too severe for harsh daylight, it's perfect for this look, which is designed to be seen in softer, sexier light! Using a pencil, carefully draw a fine line above and below your eyelashes. If you find it hard to create a steady line, try drawing a series of tiny dots, then blend them together with a clean cotton bud (swab).

5 Tawny blusher or a bronzing powder is ideal for this look, as this natural colour won't compete with the rest of your make-up. Sweep it over your cheekbones, blending away the edges into your hairline.

2 Apply a little of the same eyeshadow under your lower lashes to accentuate the shape of your eyes. This will give a balanced look to your eye make-up,

4 To contrast the dark, smoky look on your eyelids, sweep a pearlized ivory shadow over your brow bones for a wide-eyed look. Apply a little at a time, building up the effect gradually. Complete the look with two coats of black mascara.

6 Keeping the lips neutral gives this look its real impact, and updates it. Opt for a pinkish-beige shade of lip pencil and smudge it over your entire mouth for a matte, understated effect.

Right: Smoky eyes and neutral lips make for a sexy, sultry look!

20 PROBLEM SOLVERS

Whether you've made a beauty mistake, have run out of a vital product or are stuck for inspiration on how to make the most of your looks, the following problem solvers are just what you need!

Problem 1

Polish remover has run out

If you want to re-paint your nails, but have run out of remover, try coating one nail at a time with a clear base coat. Leave to dry for a few seconds, then press a tissue over the nail and remove it at once – the base coat and coloured polish will come off in one quick move. Your nail is now ready for a fresh coat of colour.

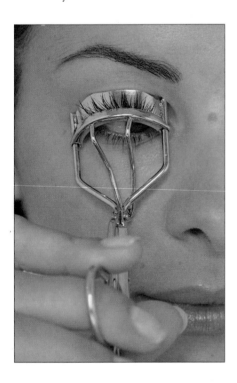

Problem 2

Poker-straight lashes

Do invest in a set of eyelash curlers, as they really make a difference to the way your eyes look. You'll never know how effective they are until you try them for the first time. Gently squeeze your lashes between their cushioned pad

Problem 3

Patchy powder

Provided you apply your powder with a light touch to freshly moisturized skin or on top of foundation that's applied with a clean sponge, it should look perfect. Check you're not making the common mistake of using the wrong colour powder for your skin. It needs to be matched closely to your natural skin-tone, as closely as your foundation. So, try dusting a sample of powder onto your skin in natural daylight before buying it, to make sure you've bought the perfect match for you.

Problem 4

Yellow nails

Yellow nails are usually caused by wearing dark-coloured nail polish without using a protective clear base coat, so wear one in future to prevent this from happening. You can also try switching to paler coloured polishes, as these contain lower levels of pigment that are less likely to stain your nails.

To cure yellow nails, rub them with lemon juice to remove the stains, then massage your hands and nails with hand cream to replenish the moisture levels. Try going polish free one day a week. If your problem recurs, consult your doctor to check that there's no underlying cause.

Problem 5

Flaky mascara

This usually means the mascara is too old and the oils that give it a creamy consistency have dried out. This can be made worse by pumping air into the dispenser when replacing the cap – so go gently. Replace your mascara every few months.

You can try to revive an old mascara by dropping it into a glass of warm water for a few minutes before applying it. If mascara flakes on your lashes, the only solution is to remove it thoroughly and to make a clean start.

Problem 6

A blemish appears

The immediate solution is to transform the blemish into a beauty mark! Start by calming down the blemish by dabbing it with a gentle astringent on a clean cotton bud (swab). This will help dry out excess oils from the skin and make the beauty mark stay in place for longer. To create your beauty mark dot over the top with an eyebrow pencil – this is better than using an eyeliner pencil as it has a drier texture and so is less likely to melt and smudge. Finally, set your beauty mark in place with a light dusting of loose powder.

Problem 8

Smudged eyeliner

Tidy up the under-eye area by dipping a cotton bud (swab) into some eye make-up remover. Whisk it over the problem area to remove smudges, then re-powder. In future, remember to run a little loose powder over eyeliner to combat the smudging that occurs when the wax in the pencil melts.

Problem 7

Melting lipstick

If you're out and about, and your lipstick is starting to move in the heat, then dust over the top with a little loose powder. This will give it a slightly drier texture, to help it stay put for longer. A little loose powder will also create a lovely matte finish.

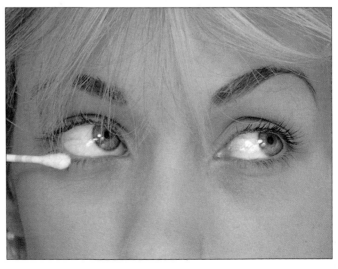

Problem 9

Red-toned skin or embarrassing blushes

A red skin colour can be toned down by smoothing your skin with a specialized green-tinted foundation. Apply with a light touch, just to the areas that really need it. The green pigment in the cream has the effect of cancelling out the red in your skin.

However, to avoid a ghostly glow, you'll need to apply a light coating of your ordinary foundation on top, and then set with a dusting of loose powder. This tip is also good for covering the occasional angry spot or blemish.

Problem 10

Foundation has turned orange

This tip sounds strange, but really works! Mix a spoonful of bicarbonate of soda into your loose face powder, then dust the powder mixture lightly over your skin before applying your foundation. The bicarbonate of soda will give your skin a slightly acid pH-balance to prevent it from turning orange.

Problem 11

Bleeding lipstick

Use lipliner to prevent your lipstick from bleeding into the fine lines around your mouth. Trace the lip outline, then apply lip colour with a brush. Choose a drier textured matte lipstick as they're less prone to bleed than moisturizing variety. Also, lightly powder over and around your lips before you start.

Problem 12

Disappearing foundation

If your foundation seems to sink into your skin on hot or damp days, then rethink how you apply it in the first place. The trick to help foundation last longer is to apply it to cool skin. Do this by holding a cold, damp facecloth onto your skin for a few moments, then apply your foundation.

You can also store your foundation in the refrigerator to ensure it's cool when it goes on. Apply the foundation with a damp sponge, not your fingers, as the natural oils from them will leave a streaky finish on your skin. Finally, set with a light dusting of loose powder.

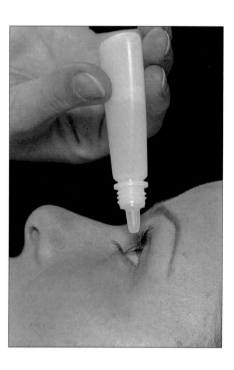

Problem 13

Bloodshot eyes

Red eyes are caused by the swelling of the tiny blood vessels on the eye surface, which can be caused by lack of sleep, excessive time in front of a computer, a smoky atmosphere or an infection. If it's a continual problem, consult your doctor, or ask your optician for an eyesight examination to ensure there's nothing to worry about.

Also, take care to avoid the source of the problem in future. On a temporary basis, you can use eye drops to bring the sparkle back to your eyes. These contain ingredients to reduce the swelling in the blood vessels that will decrease redness and cut down on dryness and itching.

Problem 14

Tidemarks of foundation

If you find obvious edges to your foundation on your chin, jawline or hairline, blend them away with a damp cosmetic sponge. Do this in natural daylight so you can check the finished effect. Powder as usual afterwards.

Problem 17

Droopy eyes

To help lift the appearance of droopy eyes, sweep a light-toned eyeshadow all over your eyelid. Then apply a little eye-shadow with a clean cotton bud (swab) under your eyes, sweeping it slightly upwards. Apply extra coats of mascara on the lashes just above the iris of the eye to draw attention to the centre of your eye rather than the outer corners.

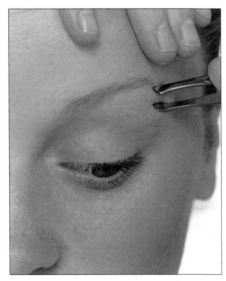

Problem 15

Unhealthy looking nails

Sometimes, however strong your nails are, their overall effect can be spoilt by clear or yellowing tips. However, you can immediately improve them by running a white manicure pencil underneath the free edges of nail to give them a cleaner appearance. Combine with a coat of clear polish for a fresh, natural nail look.

Problem 16

Yellow Teeth

First of all, consult your dentist or dental hygienist for regular check-ups and thorough cleaning to ensure your teeth are as white as possible. Take heart that yellow teeth tend to be stronger than their whiter counterparts! To make them look whiter, avoid coral or brown-based lipsticks as the warm colours will emphasize the yellow ones in your teeth. Clear pink or red shades will make them look much whiter in comparison.

Problem 18

Straggly eyebrows

It's a fair bet you won't even notice your eyebrows until they look messy! Try tidying them with regular tweezing sessions. The ideal time is after a bath, when your pores will be open from the heat, so the hairs will be easier to remove. Before bedtime is also a great idea, so you don't have to face the day with reddened skin!

Quickly brush your brows into place, so you can see the natural shape. Then pluck one hair at a time, in the direction of growth. First remove the hairs between your brows, and then weed out the undereye area. Tweeze any stray hairs at the outer sides. As a general rule, don't pluck above the eyebrow area or you'll risk distorting the shape of your brows. The only exception is if there are hairs growing well above the natural browline.

Problem 19

Over-applied blusher

If you've forgotten the golden rule about building up your blusher slowly and gradually, you may need to tone down an over-enthusiastic application of colour. The quickest and easiest way is to dust a little loose powder over the top of the problem area, until you've reached a depth of blusher shade that you're happy with.

Problem 20

Sore ears from cheap earrings

If you can't bear to throw away cheap earrings that make your ears react, try coating the posts and back of the earrings with some hypo-allergenic clear nail polish. This will make them less likely to react with your sensitive skin. However, always give the skin on your ears time to heal up before wearing troublesome earrings again.

HANDS UP TO BEAUTIFUL NAILS

A little manual labour is all it takes to have hands to be proud of – rather than ones you want to hide!

LAYING THE FOUNDATIONS FOR HEALTHY NAILS

There's no point in slicking your nails with colour if they're not in good condition to start with. Following this advice will ensure they're ultra-tough.

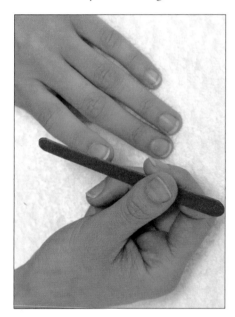

Filing know how

Keep your nails slightly square or oval – not pointed – to prevent them from breaking. Filing low into the corners and sides can weaken nails. File gently in one long stroke, from the side to the centre of the nail. The classic length that suits most hands is just over the fingertip.

Condition-plus

Smooth your nails every evening with a nourishing oil or conditioning cream. This helps seal moisture into your nails to prevent flaking and splitting. A tiny drop of olive oil is a great cheap alternative.

Cuticle care

Go carefully with tough or overgrown cuticles. Most manicurists are against cutting them with scissors, as this can lead to infection of the nail bed. Instead, soak your nails in warm soapy water to soften

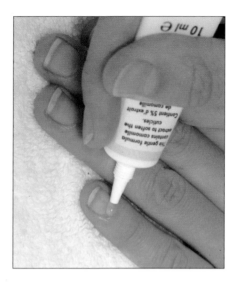

the cuticles. Then smooth them with a little cuticle softening cream or gel, before gently pushing them back with a manicure hoof stick or clean cotton bud (swab). You can then gently scrub away the flakes of dead skin that are still clinging to the nail bed.

Above: Give your nails a splash of colour for instant glamour.

POLISH UP YOUR FRENCH!

When it comes to nail trends, there's one look that never goes out of fashion, and that's the French manicure. It leaves your nails looking clean, fresh and healthy – and matches any make-up you happen to be wearing.

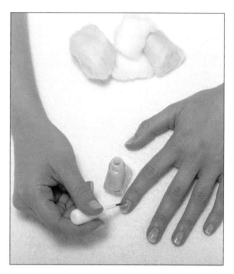

1 The basis of the French manicure is two coats of pale pink polish. Copy the professionals and do it in three strokes – one down the middle and one on each side. This prevents the polish from going lumpy and clogging, as you don't continuously have to work over the same area of nail. Apply two coats, giving each one plenty of time to dry. To turn a French manicure into an "American manicure", switch the pink polish for a beige one.

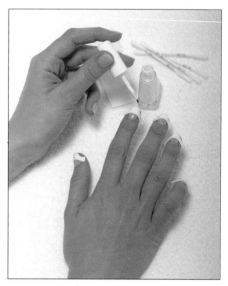

2 Now it's time to paint the tips of your nails with a white polish. If you find it difficult to paint them freehand, try using the stick-on nail guards that come with many French manicure sets. Simply press them onto the nail bed,

leaving the free edges of nail clear. Then apply the white polish, being careful not to overload the brush or the varnish will flow down it too quickly for you to control. Rest your hand on a firm surface to keep your hands steady and create a professional-looking finish.

3 Once the white tips of your nails are dry, paint on a clear top coat of polish to seal in the colour and create a chip-free finish.

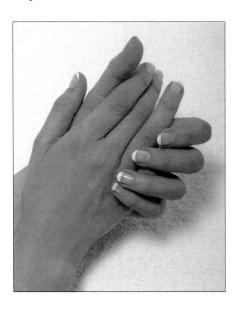

Above: French polish your nails to make them look clean and fresh.

COLOUR CODING

● If you have long, elegant fingers, you can carry off any shade of polish, including the dramatic deep reds, russets and burgundies.

● Short nails look their best with pale or beige-toned polish.

● Pale colours also suit broad nails. However, you can make them look slightly narrower by leaving a little space on the sides of each nail unpainted.

● If you love nude, barely-there shades for the daytime, but prefer something more exotic at night, try a pale pearlized polish – the shimmer will be caught by the evening light.

● If you find strong colours too bold on

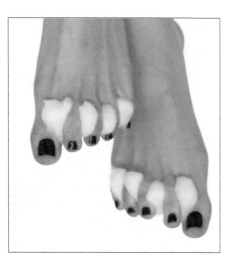

your hands, try painting your toenails instead. A glimpse of wonderful colour in open-toed shoes or on bare feet can look very sophisticated. You can create our model look by mixing a little dark red and black nail polish together before applying.

● Coral polish and pearlized formulations work wonderfully against a tanned skin.

TOP 10 NAIL TIPS

1 Avoid using acetone nail polish removers, as these can strip your nails of essential moisture. Choose the conditioning variety, instead.

2 Apply hand cream every time you wash your hands. The oils in the cream will seal moisture into your nails.

3 The most common cause of soft nails is exposure to water, so wear rubber gloves when doing the dishes!

4 If you have very weak nails, try painting your base coat and nail polish under the tip of your nails to give them extra strength.

5 Dry wet nails in an instant by plunging them into ice cold water.

6 To repair a split nail, tear a little paper from a teabag or coffee filter paper and glue it over the tear with nail glue. Once it's dry, buff until smooth, and then apply your polish.

7 If you're planning to do some gardening or messy work, drag your nails over a bar of soap. The undersides of your nails will fill up with soap, which means dirt won't be able to get in.

8 Clean ink and stains from your fingertips, by using a toothbrush and toothpaste on the affected areas.

9 Never file your nails immediately after a bath, as this is when they're at their weakest and likely to split.

10 Use a cotton bud (swab) with a pointed end to clean under your nails – it's gentler than scrubbing with a nail brush.

50 FAST, EFFECTIVE BEAUTY TIPS

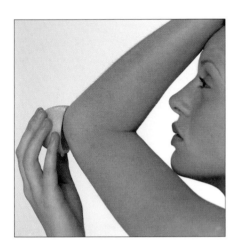

1 Brighten grey elbows by rubbing them with half a fresh lemon – it has a natural bleaching effect. Moisturize the skin afterwards to counteract the drying effects of the juice.

2 Turn foundation into a tinted moisturizer by mixing a few drops of it with a little moisturizer on the back of your hand before applying. It's the perfect blend for summer.

3 Carry a spray of mineral water in your handbag to freshen up your foundation while you're out and about.

4 Sleeping on your back helps stop wrinkles, according to recent research. It's certainly worth a try!

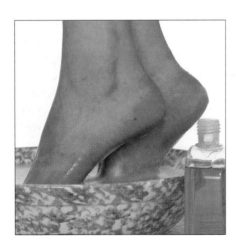

5 Dunk feet into a bowl containing warm water and 4 tablespoons of Epsom salts to help ease swollen ankles.

6 If you have very soft nails, file them while the polish is still on to prevent them from cracking.

7 If you find eyebrow tweezing painful, hold an ice cube over the area first to numb the area before you start.

8 Warm up your looks by dusting a little blusher over your temples, chin and the tip of your nose as well as your cheeks.

9 Sweep a little loose powder under your eyes when applying dark shades of eyeshadow to catch any falling specks and prevent them from staining your skin.

10 Make your lips look larger by wearing a bright, light lipstick. Make them appear smaller by wearing dark or more muted colours.

11 Soak nails in a bowl of olive oil once a week to strengthen them.

12 Keep your smile looking its best by changing your toothbrush as soon as the bristles begin to splay. This means at least every three months. You should brush for at least two minutes, both morning and evening.

13 If you don't have a specialized contouring product for your cheeks, simply use an ordinary face powder a couple of shades darker than your usual one to slim round cheeks.

14 Add a drop of witch hazel – available from all good pharmacists – to turn ordinary foundation into a medicated one – it'll work wonders on oily or blemish-prone skins.

15 Mascara your lashes before applying false ones to help them stick properly.

16 If you look tired, blend a little concealer just away from the outer corner of your eye – it makes you look as though you had a good night's sleep!

17 Go lightly with powder on wrinkles around the eyes – too much will settle into them and emphasize them.

18 If you haven't got time for a full make-up, but want to look great, paint on a bright red lipstick – it's a happy, glamorous colour which immediately brightens your face.

19 When plucking your eyebrows, coat the hairs you want to remove with concealer – it'll help you visualize exactly the shape of brow you're after.

20 Never apply your make-up before blow-drying your hair – the heat from the dryer can make you perspire and cause your make-up to smudge.

21 The colour of powder eyeshadow can be made to look more intense by dipping your eyeshadow brush in water first.

22 Keep lashes smooth and supple by brushing them with petroleum jelly before going to bed at night. It's also a good way to emphasize natural-looking lashes in the daytime.

23 Apply cream blusher in light downward movements, to prevent it from creasing and specks of colour from catching in the fine hairs on your face.

24 If mascara tends to clog on your lower lashes, try using a small thin brush to paint colour onto individual lashes.

25 Make sure you give moisturizer time to sink in before you start applying your make-up – it'll help your make-up go on more easily.

26 For eyes that really sparkle, try outlining them just inside your lower eyelashes with a soft white cosmetic pencil.

27 Lip gloss can look sophisticated if you apply just a dot in the centre of your lower lip.

28 Hide cracked or chipped nails under stick-on false ones.

29 If your eyeliner is too hard and drags your skin, hold it next to a light bulb for a few seconds before applying.

30 If you find your lashes clog with mascara, try rolling the brush in a tissue first to blot off the excess, leaving a light, manageable film on the bristles.

31 If you're unsure where to apply blusher, gently pinch your cheeks. If you like the effect, apply blusher in the same area – it'll look wonderfully natural.

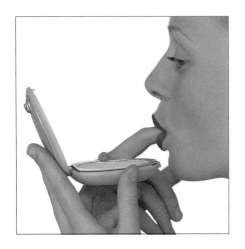

32 To prevent lipstick from getting on your teeth, try this tip: after putting it on, put your finger in your mouth, purse your lips and pull it out.

33 Women who wear glasses need to take special advice on make-up. If you're nearsighted, your glasses will make your eyes look smaller. So, opt for brighter, bolder shadows and lots of mascara to ensure they don't disappear. If you're far-sighted, your lenses will make your eyes look bigger and your eye make-up more prominent. So, opt for more muted colours that won't seem so obvious.

34 For a long-lasting blush on sunny days or hot nights, apply both cream and powder blusher. Apply the cream formulation

first, set with translucent powder then dust with a little powder blush.

35 Let your nails breathe by leaving a tiny gap at the base of the nail where the cuticle meets the nail – this is where the new nail cells are growing.

36 A little foundation lightly rubbed through your eyebrows and brushed through with an old toothbrush will instantly lighten them.

37 Coloured mascara can look supereffective if applied with a light hand. Start by coating your lashes with two coats of black mascara. Once the lashes are dry, slick a little coloured mascara – try blue, violet or green – onto the underside of your upper lashes. Each time you blink your eyelashes will reveal a dash of unexpected colour.

38 If you use hypo-allergenic make-up for your sensitive skin, remember to use hypo-allergenic nail polish, too – you constantly touch your face with your hands and can easily trigger a reaction.

39 Make over-prominent eyes appear smaller by applying a wide coat of liquid liner. The thicker the line, the smaller your eyes will look.

40 Calm down an angry red blemish by holding an ice cube over it for a few seconds and then apply your usual medicated concealer.

41 If you've run out of loose powder, use a light dusting of unperfumed talcum powder instead.

42 Use a little green eyeshadow on red eyelids to mask the ruddiness.

43 If you've run out of liquid eyeliner, dip a thin brush into your mascara and apply in the same way. It works perfectly.

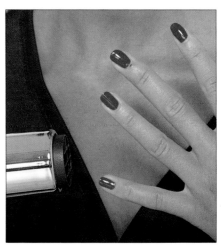

44 You can dry nail polish quickly by blasting nails with a cold jet of air from your hairdryer.

45 Use a toothpick or dental floss regularly to clean between your teeth.

46 Apply powder-foundation with a damp sponge for a thicker, more opaque coverage. Applied with a dry sponge, the effect will be sheerer.

47 Run your freshly sharpened eyeliner pencil across a tissue before use. This will round off any sharp edges and remove small particles of wood.

48 If you have hard-to-cover under-eye shadows, cover them with a light coat of blue cream eyeshadow before using your ordinary concealer. It really works.

49 Get together with a friend and make each other up – it's amazing how other people picture you – and it's a great way to find yourself a new look.

50 Remove excess mascara by placing a folded tissue between your upper and lower lashes and then blinking two or three times.

50 BEST BUDGET BEAUTY TIPS

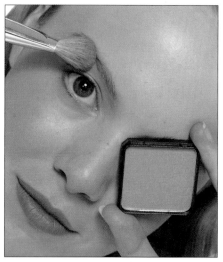

12 Dust blusher over your eyelids as an instant subtle eyeshadow. It's quick to apply, and will give a balanced look to your make-up.

13 Rub a dab of petroleum jelly around the neck of a new nail polish bottle, and it should be easy to open for the entire life of the product.

14 A cheap way to boost the shine of dark hair is to rinse it with diluted vinegar. Blonde hair benefits from lemon juice. Both act by sealing down the outer cuticles of the hair, helping your hair reflect the light more effectively.

15 De-fuzz using a razor with replaceable blades – it works out much cheaper in the end than buying disposable razors.

16 Swap commercial face scrubs for a handful of oatmeal massaged directly onto your skin – it works really well.

17 Don't use too much toothpaste – it's the brushing action that gets teeth really clean. A pea-sized blob is enough.

18 Pick the largest sized products you can afford – it's much cheaper that way.

19 Don't just shop for beauty goodies in glitzy department stores and fancy pharmacies. These days, your local supermarket can offer a surprisingly good range.

20 If you're happy to forgo a fancy label, look out for great value own-label product ranges at leading drug store chains.

21 Sometimes you're just as well off with cheap alternatives. Opt for those when you can, and indulge yourself with the

1 Cottonwool (cotton) balls soak up liquids like toner, so dampen them with water first. Squeeze out the excess, then use as usual.

2 A drop of remover added to a bottle of dried-up nail polish will revive it in a few seconds. Shake well to encourage it to mix in thoroughly.

3 Stand a dried-up mascara in a glass of warm water to bring it back to life.

4 Keep new soaps from getting too soft by putting them in a warm cupboard until you need them. This helps dry the moisture out, which makes them harder and longer-lasting.

5 To get the last drop out of almost-empty bottles store them upside-down overnight. You'll reap the rewards the next morning.

6 Don't rip the cellophane cover off translucent powder – prick a few holes in it instead – it'll stop you spilling and wasting it.

7 Keep perfume strips from magazines in your bag for an instant freshen-up.

8 Sachets in magazines make ideal travel packs for weekends away.

9 If you've run out of blusher, dot a little pink lipstick on your cheeks and blend well with your fingertips.

10 Look out for "2 for the price of 1" special offers on your favourite products. Perhaps split the savings with a friend.

11 Turn ordinary mascara into the lash-lengthening variety by dusting eyelashes with a little translucent powder first.

products that are really worth it! For instance, buy cheap and cheerful lip liners, then show off with a fancy lipstick. As well as looking good, expensive lipsticks tend to contain more pigment than cheaper ones – which means they look better and last longer.

22 Buy cheap but effective body moisturizers instead of expensive fragranced ones. Then save your money to splash out on your favourite perfume.

23 It used to be that only the pricier ranges offered hi-tech products. However, these days more companies are offering state-of-the-art products – at budget prices. This means you'll get all the benefits without spending a fortune. For instance, there are now affordable skin creams that contain the anti-ageing alpha-hydroxy ingredients at a third or quarter of the price of prestige brands.

24 Many of the more expensive prestige make-up, skin-care and fragrance companies offer sample products at their counters. It's generally at the discretion of the consultant. However, it's always worth asking, especially if you're already buying something from them.

25 There's a great trend at the moment for 2-in-1 products. They're worth trying, because they can save you money – as you only buy one product instead of two. They include shower gels with added moisturizers, shower gels that also act as body scrubs and hair shampoos with built in conditioners.

26 If you want to indulge in some new make-up, then ask for a makeover at a cosmetic counter. It's the best way to see how the colours and formulations look on your skin before you buy anything – and can also mean you'll look great for an evening out!

27 Store your make-up and fragrance in a cool dark place to extend their life span.

28 One length hair with no layers is the easiest and cheapest hairstyle to maintain as it doesn't require as many visits to the hairdresser to keep it looking good.

29 Don't throw away an item of make-up just because the colour's not in fashion at the moment – you might like it again in a few months.

30 Make cheap nail polish last longer by sealing it with a clear top coat.

31 Pure glycerine is an extremely cheap and effective moisturizer when you don't have much to spend.

32 Turn lipstick into lip gloss with a coat of lip balm after applying colour.

33 Double up your lip liner to fill in your lips as well as outline them.

34 Prise eyeshadows out of their cases, and stick into an old paint-box or lid to create a make-up artist's colour palette. It's a sure way to ensure you use the products you've got because you can see them all at a glance.

35 Add a few drops of your favourite eau de toilette to some olive oil, and use as a scented bath oil as a cheap treat.

36 Neutral make-up colours are a better investment than brighter ones because they look great at any time, any place.

37 Eyeshadow doubles up as eyeliner, if applied with a cotton bud (swab). Dampen the end of the bud (swab) first for a more dramatic effect.

38 If you're choosing a new fragrance, buy the weaker and cheaper eau de toilette first before splashing out on the stronger and more expensive perfume strength.

39 Check out the model nights at your local hairdressers when trainee hairdressers will style your hair for a fraction of the normal price.

40 Mix different colour lipsticks on the back of your hand with a brush – to create new shades for free!

41 A drop of olive oil rubbed nightly into your nails will help them grow long and strong, and is cheaper than shop-bought manicure oils.

42 When you're out of toothpaste, brush with plain baking soda – it'll make them extra white, too.

43 Put your lip and eye pencils in the refrigerator before sharpening, as this means they're less likely to break – and you won't waste so much.

44 Make powder eyeshadows last longer and stay crease-free by dusting eyelids with translucent powder first. It'll absorb the oils from your skin, and keep your make-up looking fresh.

45 Sharpen dull eyebrow tweezers by rubbing sandpaper along the tips.

46 Add a drop of water to the last remains of a foundation to ensure you use every last dot.

47 Keep the plastic seals or paper discs that come with products and replace after each use. It helps prevent air from distributing in the product and bacteria breeding – which means your product stays fresh until the very end.

48 Spritz your hair lightly with water and re-blow dry to revive products already in the hair, and make your style look as good as new.

49 Add half a cup of baking soda to your bath water as a cheap and cheerful water softener in hard water areas.

50 Use an old clean toothbrush to slick unruly eyebrows into shape.

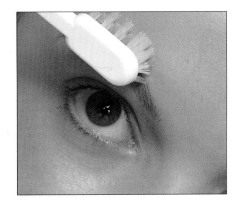

YOUR TOP 10 MAKE-UP QUESTIONS

1 Blush baby

Q *"Can I reshape my face using blusher?"*

A The best way to apply blusher is to smile, find the apples of your cheeks, and blend the colour upwards. For special occasions, try using your normal blusher – combined with a barely-there highlighter colour and a colour that is slightly darker than your usual blusher – to reshape your face. Check your face shape and try the following:

● **Slim a round face...** by blending your usual blusher upwards from your cheeks into your hairline. Then, highlight along

your cheekbones, and use the shader in the hollows of your cheeks.

● **Soften a square-shaped face...** by concentrating your blusher in a circle on the rounded parts of your cheeks. Apply shader into the hollows of your cheeks, and also lightly on the square edges of your chin. Lightly dust highlighter onto the bridge of your nose and the tip of your chin.

● **Balance a heart-shaped face...** by dusting your blusher slightly lower than your cheekbones into the actual hollows of your cheeks. Dust some highlighter onto the tip of your chin, and apply shader to your temples, blending it well into your hairline.

2 24-hour lipstick

Q *"Is there any way to make my lipstick stay put all day?"*

A Unfortunately there's no such thing as a 24-hour lipstick, no matter what some cosmetic manufacturers claim! The longest lasting lipsticks are those with the thickest, driest textures, although this can mean they leave your lips feeling quite dry, especially if you use them day in, day out. However, you can look for lipstick sealers, which are clear gels that you paint over your lips after you've applied your lipstick. Once they're dry, these lipstick sealers help your lipstick stay put at least past your first cup of coffee of the day.

3 Over-plucked brows

Q *"I plucked my eyebrows very thin last year. Now I'd like to grow them back. How can I do it successfully?"*

A Choose a natural-looking brown eyeshadow. Then apply it lightly and evenly with a firm-bristled eyebrow brush, using short sharp strokes across the brow. As the hairs that grow back are often unruly, a light coat of clear mascara can be applied to help keep them in place.

Try to ignore the periodic fashions for highly plucked eyebrows. The fashions don't last for long – but eyebrows can take ages to grow back! It's better to stick with the eyebrow shape you were born with, concentrating on just removing stray hairs from underneath the arch and between the brows.

4 Covering birthmarks

Q *"Can you recommend something that will cover my birthmark, even when I go swimming?"*

A You need a specialized foundation that will give ultimate coverage, look opaque and be waterproof. Look for a specialized range of camouflage creams tailor-made to cover skin imperfections, such as scars and port wine stains, as well as birthmarks. Their formulation means that they're applied differently to ordinary foundations. They're applied with the fingertips using a "dab, pat" motion. They're available from specialized make-up suppliers, and some dermatologists.

5 Spider Veins

Q *" What can I do about the spider veins on my face?"*

A Spider or thread veins, known by their medical name as "telangiectases", are a very common beauty problem. An electrolysist qualified in diathermy or a dermatologist can treat them for you, by inserting a very fine needle into the vein. The heat from the needle coagulates the blood inside the vein, rendering it inactive. The number of treatments varies depending on the size of the area to be treated, and the number of spider veins you have. In the meantime, you can cover the veins with a light covering of concealer, applied with a fine brush and set with a dusting of loose powder.

6 Mascara matters

Q *"My mascara always seems to run onto my skin, and leave me with 'panda eyes'. What can I do?"*

A Obviously you should opt for the waterproof variety of mascara if you're prone to this problem, or you can "seal" your normal mascara with a coat of clear mascara. You should also try holding a piece of tissue just underneath your lower lashes while you're applying your mascara to prevent it from getting as far as your skin in the first place.

Alternatively, dip a cotton bud (swab) in eye make-up remover for fast touch-ups before the mascara has a moment to dry on your skin. Another, more long-term, solution is to regularly have your eyelashes permanently dyed at a reputable beauty salon.

7 Colour coding

Q *"Are there colours which some people can never wear?"*

A As a general rule, everyone can wear every colour. However, if you want to wear a particular colour, you should choose the particular shade of it very carefully. For instance, everyone can wear red lipstick, but in different shades. A pale-skinned blonde will suit a soft pink-red, whereas a warm-toned redhead will be able to carry off an orange-based fiery shade of the colour.

In the same way, a blue-eyed, cool-skinned blonde can carry off a pale pastel, baby blue eyeshadow, whereas her brunette colleague will look much better wearing a darker version to complement her skin-tone.

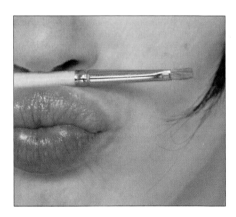

8 Smoother lips

Q *"Lipstick always looks awful on my mouth because my lips are so flaky, and it's impossible to create a smooth finish. Is there a solution to this problem?"*

A Slick your lips with petroleum jelly, and leave for 10 minutes to give it time to soften hard flakes of skin. Then cover your index finger with a damp flannel and gently massage your lips. This will remove the petroleum jelly and the flakes of dead skin at the same time.

9 Problem polish

Q *"I always seem to be left with lots of bottles of nail varnish which I can't use, because they're either dried up, or full of bubbles which means they don't go on smoothly. What can I do?"*

A There are some simple solutions to your problem. Dried-up polish can be revived by stirring in a few drops of polish remover before using. You can help prevent it from thickening in the first place by storing it in the refrigerator, as the cold temperature will stem evaporation and thereby stop it changing in texture.

Bubbles of air in the polish will ruin its finish, as it won't create an even surface. You can prevent this by rolling the bottle between the palms of your hands to mix it up before using, rather than shaking it vigorously – as it's this which creates the bubbles in the first place.

10 The changing face of foundation

Q *"I have difficulty keeping up with the changing colour of my skin in the summer, as I gradually get a tan. It's so expensive constantly buying new foundations!"*

A Stick with the the colour that suits you when you're at your palest in the middle of winter. Then, also buy a small tube of dark foundation designed for black skins. Blend just a drop or two into your ordinary foundation on the back of your hand before applying to darken it to match your tan. This means you can change your foundation daily, without having to spend a fortune on different shades.

INDEX